Zell J. Schulman is a culinary consultant, cooking instructor, and food columnist. She has been a guest chef and lecturer on numerous television shows and made personal appearances throughout the Cincinnati area for over ten years. Her column, "The Modern Jewish Holiday Cook" is a regular feature in *The American Israelite*.

Mrs. Schulman is a board member of both the National Campaign for the United Jewish Appeal as well as the National Women's Board of the United Jewish Appeal. She is also a member of the Executive Committee of the Board of the Women's Division of the Jewish Federation of Cincinnati. In 1979 she was selected as Woman of the Year by B'nai B'rith in Cincinnati.

She has received her formal cooking training under Richard Grausman of Le Cordon Bleu de Paris, and in selected classes with Abbey Mandel, Carl Jerome, and Giuliano Bugialli.

birmingham alabama what's cooking in birmingham phoenix arizona eat and
pepper to taste berkeley california the berkeley jewish cookbook beverly hills
beverly hills california from noodles to strudles castro valley california what's c
california flavored with love palo alto california favorite recipes san diego cali
california delectable collectable   nda second helpings, please! r
health stamford connectic   hartford connecticut passo
leavened with love clear   daytona beach florida m
florida food for thoug   vorite recipes balabu
hallandale florida d   ily favorites hollyw
gourmet delights i   ksonville florida tr
this and kosher t   allahassee floric
jewish dishes a'   happy cooker a
kitchen chicac   the fort sheri
cookbook wil   a the cooker
recipes dave   na kitchen t
louisiana fr   ook potom
massachus   nought coc
center tab'   abody ma
sudbury n   ts the ha
arbor mic   e mama
magic oa'   e afraid t
treats col   neration
council's   garden
inois wo   kery ce
va specia   en treat
essen 'n   sey to s∈
jersey lo   on new
new mexi   iew york
bingham   s brookl
kosher je   new yor
new york t   m our be
elegant es: om dora v
enjoy malv   itchen ma
inspirations   ew york nev
plainview ne   k favorite re
hadassah coo   ring valley ne
island new yor   s choice west I
spice charlotte r.   favorite recipe:
cleveland ohio fai   e sport of cookir
kitchen cincinnati c   chef bala cynwyd p
havertown pennslyva   ylvania plotz and par
with love philadelphia p   terhood cookbook sta
women of brit shalom wyi   ck and easy cookbook ch:
charleston with love charleston   storically speaking columbia
blountville tennessee recipes by request bryan texas favorite recipes dallas te
arthur texas bicentennial cookbook danville virginia favorite recipes from our
from soup to nosh lynchburg virginia kitchen knishes newport news virginia a
virginia try it you'll like it parkersburg west virginia season to taste milwaukee w

Something
Different
for
Passover

Zell J. Schulman

TRIAD PUBLISHING COMPANY   GAINESVILLE, FLORIDA

Books in The Chosen Cookbook Series

The Chosen: Appetizers & Deserts
Jewish Cooking Made Slim
Quick & Easy
Something Different for Passover

Library of Congress Cataloging in Publication Data

Schulman, Zell, 1928–
Something different for Passover.

(The Chosen cookbook series)
Includes index.
1. Cookery, Jewish. 2. Passover cookery. I. Title.
II. Series.
TX724.S33 1985   641.5′676   85–28963
ISBN 0–937404–24–1 (pbk.)

© 1986 by Zell Schulman
Cover artwork © 1986 by Triad Publishing Company

Printed in the United States of America

Published and distributed by Triad Publishing Company, Inc.
1110 Northwest Eighth Avenue
Gainesville, Florida 32601

The recipes for Carrot and Sweet Potato Tzimmes, page 105, Matzo Brie, page 116, Passover Fudge Squares, page 169, and some of the information in Tips on Using Your Food Processor are adapted from *Quick & Easy*, by Shelley Melvin. © 1984 by Triad Publishing Company.

Most Triad books are available at special quantity discounts for bulk purchases for sales promotions, premiums, or fundraising. For details contact Special Sales Department, Triad Publishing Company, 1110 Northwest Eighth Avenue, Gainesville, Florida 32601.

To my friends and family

Contents

Foreword

"In every generation, each person should feel as though she or he were redeemed from Egypt."

The Haggadah

And so, we prepare ourselves and our households for Passover, for that process of redemption that we re-experience every year.

Preparations for Passover take place in many ways. We clean our houses and get rid of any chametz, that mixture of flour and water that has risen. Not just our homes need to be cleaned. We clean or change our utensils, dishes, and pots and pans as well. For the process of making something "Kosher l' Pesach" is much stricter than the process of making it kosher for everyday use—either it is "Kosher l' Pesach" or it is "Hametzdik." Therefore, the physical preparation can be quite time-consuming or at times seem cumbersome.

Some of us enjoy the chance to clean out everything and see it as a spring cleaning ritual. There are ways to get our whole family involved in the process, so that even young children feel that they have had a part in helping make their home ready. At the same time, we need to be careful not to get so bogged down in cleaning that we lose sight of other spiritual or religious significance that the holiday has to offer.

For Passover is a holiday of renewal, of the rebirth of ourselves as a people. It forces us to remember the time when the people of Israel were slaves and when we were brought out of oppression and enslavement in Egypt. That significant historical event shaped not only those in the generation that left Egypt, it has affected all subsequent generations of Jews, in their struggles to be free people, individually and as a nation. Even though we did not know what difficulties freedom would entail or how hard the journey would be, we were ready to leave everything behind and embark on that journey.

We celebrate that exodus not just by getting rid of the chametz, but by bringing new ideas, symbols, ceremonies, and foods into our lives. Some of the preparations and symbols are the same each year. But we also look forward to each Passover being a bit different from the previous Passovers we have experienced, just as *we* change from year to year.

There are ways to bring the old and new together in a Seder meal. In some households, all the participants, children as well as adults, are asked to bring some idea or story to contribute to the Seder. In our house, we do not just read the four questions. We feel free to bring up additional questions that we ourselves are now asking. We recognize that there is a part of each of the four types of children in each of us.

It is this blending of the old and new, the known and the yet-to-be-experienced that is part of Passover. And that applies just as much to the foods we eat during the holiday. We serve some traditional favorites year after year because they remind us of those special Seder meals we ate as children. But we're also open to trying new things and experimenting with new recipes, with new ways to prepare meals from the same ingredients we have had in our Passover kitchens for years.

It is, therefore, the perfect time to try a new cookbook. That way, we are not "enslaved" to repetition and habit. Instead, we can learn new ways to make our enjoyment of this important holiday even greater.

JOANNE SCHINDLER

Preface

Every Spring, when I check my calendar and see the word "Passover" written in its assigned square, I always tell myself, "This year Passover will be different." When I was growing up, watching my grandmother Jacobs cooking and preparing her home for the holiday played a very important part in the feeling I developed and the many traditions I established for Passover. Each year, we look forward to the Seders, retelling, with recitation, commentary, and song, the story of the Jews' flight from Egypt to freedom. Melvin and I look at the faces of our children, grandson, inlaws, nieces, nephews, and friends sitting around our Passover table, and have a feeling of love, accomplishment, and hope.

I have prepared more cooking classes for this holiday than any other. Weeks in advance, I begin ordering the meat and poultry, shopping for groceries, and filling in the supplies I need. I unpack the Passover dishes, cookware, and glasses and get them ready for the holiday week. It is always a special time for me.

This is the one week of the year when all our meals will be eaten at home. No restaurants, taking the children to a drive-in, or meeting my friends for a quick bite. This holiday is one where my culinary creativeness is put to the text. Thanks to today's kitchen technology, preparing new Passover dishes is easier than ever. I have the opportunity to combine the old with the new, using traditional recipes with modern methods and equipment. It is fascinating to see what I can do with my food processor and microwave oven, and yet a wonderful learning experience to know that many of the traditional dishes don't have the right "tam" (taste) if I don't stick to the conventional methods. My love of tradition, my zest for new things, and my ability to share with others have helped me make "something different for Passover."

ZELL SCHULMAN

Acknowledgements

I wish to thank those who shared their time, knowledge, and recipes with me, preparing "Something Different for Passover" Some of the original recipes were adapted for the cookbook.

Gertrude Beer
Mrs. Max Brown
Terry Barr
Karen Schulman Bear
Ora Bennet
Suellen Chesley
Patricia Corbett
Cordy (Mrs. Jean) Crowther
Debbie Fox
Esther Ganor
Edwina B. Gantz
Inge Goldberg
Margaret Green
Goldie Jean Fine
Mindy F. Hastie
Dena Jerimiahu
Rae J. Klein
Hannah Jacobs
Melissa E. Lanier
Sylvia (Mrs. Morris G.) Levin
Florence Lieberman
Cynthia R. Marver
Aaron Mathieu
Rhoda Mayerson

Margaret Minster
Bess Paper
Marilyn Reichert
Dora Roth
Maude Robertson
Yelena Rura
Alan Schulman
H. Glenn Schulman
Melvin L. Schulman
Marcella Segal
Cleo Seremetes
Marilyn Sholiton
Janice Shulman
Hazel Sylvia Solomon
Estelle Stein
Mrs. Joseph S. Stern, Sr.
Lynda Tucker
Fanny Weiner
Beatrice Winkler
Louise Wolf
Barbara G. Workman
Jane Wulsin
Vivian Zimmelman

llinois world of our flavors south bend indiana the cookery cedar rapids
wa specialties of the house alexandria louisiana kitchen treats cookboo
es to noshes lewiston maine sisterhood cookbook potomac maryland p
nelting pot lexington mass hought cookbook newton
ok norwood massachus ody massachusetts cc
etts in the best of tast e happy cooker of te
with temple beth a used to make f
igan all the recip 'o ask saint pau
ouri deborah c o generation b
rry hill new je eating east
ion new jers with love s
le tinton fa y the spice
ooking? al onderful
k cookie york the
ng brook osher ki
like it cli ast no
new yo great r
york th it vern
na had sher c
osher nester
scars what
ood ta d nev
carol d ohi
ount t nd of
io in t nia th
ania th n per
ia pen penr
n wynr south
charles rolina
e recipe) years
nial co oks fal
nchburg n good
e it parke sin from
gham alab at and en
ste berkele iills califor
california fr hat's cookir
flavored with iego californ
lectable collec ease! rockvill
d connecticut foc passover made
earwater florida cle a measures and tr
ght gainesville florid alabustas' more favo
it in the kitchen hollyw s hollywood florida nib
ksonville florida what's coo. ville florida try you'll like

Getting Ready for Passover

atellite beach florida our favorite recipes tallahassee florida knishes gefil
georgia golden soup atlanta georgia the happy cooker augusta georgi
ois portal to good cooking great lakes illinois the fort sheridan and great l

Getting Ready for Passover

You can make your holiday planning and preparation less frenzied by getting organized early. Many families begin preparing right after Purim. A series of lists of work to be done and items to be purchased is helpful, especially when you want the entire family to share in the tasks and in the satisfaction of seeing steps completed and checked off.

Since you'll have to rid the house of chametz, and since chametz may have worked its way into every corner of the house—even into household dust—a thorough housecleaning is a major element of Passover preparation. So make a list for cleaning chores and assign responsibilities early. Include items that need fixing and allow enough time for scheduling minor repairs.

Then check out your inventory of non-food Passover items and list what needs to be purchased—extra wine glasses, haggadahs, dishes, extras for your food processor (bowls, blades, covers), glass trays for your microwave, and so on.

Take an inventory of those foods in your pantry, refrigerator, and freezer that may contain chametz, such as bread, rice, corn, beans, and cereal. Plan meals around those foods so you can use up as much as possible before Passover.

Make your Seder menu and guest list. (Remember the obligation to include the lonely or unfortunate.) Then list the Passover cooking supplies you have on hand and those you need to purchase. Remember to include the items for the Seder plate. Careful planning will save you money as you stock your Passover pantry.

Write out a special-order list for Passover wines, chocolate, and candies and place your order before supplies are exhausted. If you don't live near a store that carries Passover products, you may have to rely on a friend or relative who lives in a better supplied area to shop for you. Or, you can order through your synagogue gift shop.

You may want to include shmurah matzahs in your order. These are matzahs baked by hand from grains that have been guarded from the time of harvest. They may be quite expensive, but it is a mitzvah to use them at a Seder meal, at least for the ceremonial matzah. If this matzah is not available locally, check with your synagogue about ordering.

Clean and line Passover storage cabinets early so that you'll have a place to store Passover foods. Once you have cabinet space ready, you can temporarily kosher your sink and wash and put away your Passover dishes, cookware, and utensils. You may be able to clean and line your freezer early and cover your counters, so that you can do some of your Passover baking ahead of time and store it in the Passover-ready freezer.

Make out a cooking schedule. To help you plan, I have included several sample menus and a timetable for preparation. You may select from these according to your customs and taste.

A few days before the holiday, kosher your ovens (don't forget the microwave), stove top, and sink. Clean the refrigerator thoroughly and line it, making sure cold air can still circulate. By this time, all your cabinets should have been cleaned, so you can seal away your regular dishes and utensils. Many families use convenience foods and disposable plates and utensils for the last few days before Passover.

You can set the table for the Seder two or three days ahead of time and cover it with a clean cloth or sheet to keep the dust and chametz off.

What Is Kosher for Passover?

When the Jews fled from bondage in Egypt, they departed so quickly that the dough for their bread did not have time to rise. To commemorate our ancestors' flight, we allow no leavening agents in our Passover foods.

This rule is subject to differing interpretations. For example, Sephardic Jews (from around the Mediterranean and the Middle East) serve legumes such as beans, peas, and rice at Passover. Because they used only wheat to bake their bread, they see no reason to avoid legumes on Passover. But in Europe, bread was formerly made not only from wheat but from a variety of legumes, so Ashkenanzic Jews (of Northern and Eastern European origin) do not use these ingredients in Passover cooking.

Matzah meal pancakes are not universally considered Kosher for Passover. Some Ashkenazim refuse to mix matzah derivatives with liquids because the unbaked matzah particles may be susceptible to leaven. This group allows a narrower range of foods for Passover than most other Jews. Another group eats matzah products, but only on the eighth day of Passover.

Because of these variations, I have collected and developed a broad spectrum of recipes in the hope of pleasing a wide audience. Basically, the ingredients called for fall into one of two categories: those which must be properly labeled "Kosher l' Pesach" and certified by rabbinical authority, and those which require no special labels if they are purchased in unopened packages or containers or in a natural state. If you have any doubt about whether a product is Kosher for Passover, please consult your rabbi.

Among the foods that must contain the "Kosher l' Pesach" label and be certified for Passover use by rabinical authority are:

Matzah, matzah flour, Passover noodles
Candies, cakes, cookies, jams and jellies
Cheeses, milk, and butter
Canned and processed foods, such as fruits, sauces, and soups
Salad oils, shortenings, vinegar
Beverages, wine and liquors
Vegetable gelatin
Relishes
Dried fruits
Horseradish

The following foods require no Kosher l' Pesach label if they are in unopened packages or containers or in a natural state:

Coffee, tea, and sugar (but not confectioners' sugar, because it contains cornstarch)
Salt, pepper, and spices (some herbs should be fresh)
All fruits and nuts
All vegetables except legumes such as peas, corn, and beans
Fruits and vegetables normally permitted for Passover use are permitted in their frozen state, provided they have not been cooked or processed in any way.

Chametz—foods with leavening—may not be eaten during Passover.

All grains (wheat, rye, oats, barley, rice, kasha, spelt) or any of their derivitives
Leavened bread, cakes, biscuits, crackers, and cereals, and any store bought baked goods not labeled Kosher l' Pesach
Any product with flavoring made from grain alcohol, such as vanilla extract, brandy, beer, or liquor
Legumes such as corn, beans, soy beans, lentils, lima beans, and any product made from them

Dishes and utensils

Putting away dishes, pots and pans, and utensils used during the rest of the year, and bringing out items reserved especially for Passover, heightens our sense of the sanctity of the festival week. Since most households are not stocked with a duplicate set of all kitchen items, some items may be made Kosher for Passover. You may use Passover cleanser if it is available in your area.

Pots and pans made entirely of metal and used for cooking (but not for baking) during the year must be scoured thoroughly, not used for 24 hours, and then immersed in boiling water. Pyrex dishes may be treated as metal.
Silverware made entirely of metal may be used if thoroughly scoured and immersed in boiling water.
Glassware not usually used for hot foods is traditionally made fit for Passover by soaking in water for three consecutive days, changing the water every 24 hours. The Rabbinical Assembly Committee of Jewish Law and Standards permits the use of glassware after thorough scouring.

Some kitchenware may not be made kosher for Passover.

Chinaware, pottery, all earthenware, and utensils used for baking
Utensils that may be damaged by hot water, including plastic
Knives with glued-on handles
Any vessel that cannot be thoroughly cleaned

Appliances

In general, prepare appliances by cleaning them thoroughly.

Stove or oven: Every part of the oven or stove that may have been touched by food during the year must be thoroughly cleansed and scraped. The oven and range must then be burned at maximum temperature for at least one-half hour or until the metal grids become red hot.
Dishwasher: A dishwashing machine may be used for Passover after it has been thoroughly scoured and run through one cycle empty.
Food mixer, processor, blender: These may be used if work bowls, containers, blades and beaters are new or special for Passover. All exterior surfaces must also be thoroughly cleaned.
Microwave oven: Remove the glass or plastic tray from your microwave. Wash the inside and the door. Do not use the appliance for 24 hours. Then place a 2-cup container filled with 1 cup of water in the microwave. Let this boil on high until the oven is filled with steam. If your oven comes with a glass or plastic tray, you should buy a new tray for Passover use only.
Refrigerator and freezer: Wash thoroughly and line.

The kitchen

Cabinets: Cabinets that will hold Passover dishes should be scoured with hot water, and the shelves should be covered.
Countertops. Use plastic sheets, contact paper, oilcloth, aluminum foil, or formica boards to cover counter tops.

Ingredients were available Kosher l 'Pesach at the time of writing. Manufacturers add or delete items each year, so the availability will vary.

The Search for Chametz

All chametz must be removed from the house or separated by putting into a room, closet, or cupboard that is locked. The chametz can then be formally sold to non-Jews. Because this procedure is legally intricate, a rabbi usually acts as the agent for the congregation to carry out the transaction *(Mechirat Chametz)*. Although the non-Jew does not physically claim the chametz, he has the legal right to do so.

After Passover, the rabbi purchases the chametz back from the non-Jew and returns it to the original owners, or, as we do in our family, donate it to the poor.

Since, during the year, chametz may work its way into every corner of the house and even into household dust, a thorough housecleaning is considered part of the Passover preparations.

To further insure that no chametz will be found in the house during Passover, a final, ritual search *(Bedikat Chametz)* is made after dark on the night before Passover. To add interest to the ceremony, especially for children, bread may be wrapped in a napkin and hidden around the house for family members to find. The family goes from room to room, using only a candle to light the way. Traditionally, a feather is used to brush the bits of bread into a wooden spoon.

The chametz is then tied up in a cloth along with the feather, the candle, and the spoon, and burned the next morning. There are blessings to accompany both the search for and disposal of chametz.

These procedures must be modified when the first Seder falls on Saturday evening. Please consult your rabbi for instructions.

The Seder Table

Items Needed for the Seder Plate

A. *Charoset*
Composed of chopped nuts and apples, cinnamon and wine, charoset represents the mortar used by the Jews in making bricks while they were slaves in Egypt.

B. *Zeroa*
The roasted shankbone or roasted wing of a fowl represents the sacrifice of the Paschal lamb.

C. *Beitza*
The roasted hard-cooked egg symbolizes the festival offering brought to the Temple.

D. *Moror*
The bitter herbs are represented by horseradish that has been freshly grated from the horseradish root. They symbolize the bitterness of slavery for the Jews in Egypt.

E. *Karpas*
You may use parsley or celery to represent Spring, which brings rebirth and redemption. It is dipped in salt water before it is eaten to remind us of the tears and sweat of the Jewish people in slavery.

F. *Chazereth*
On most Seder plates, there is another form of bitter herbs. It may be the root of the horseradish (ungrated) or watercress.

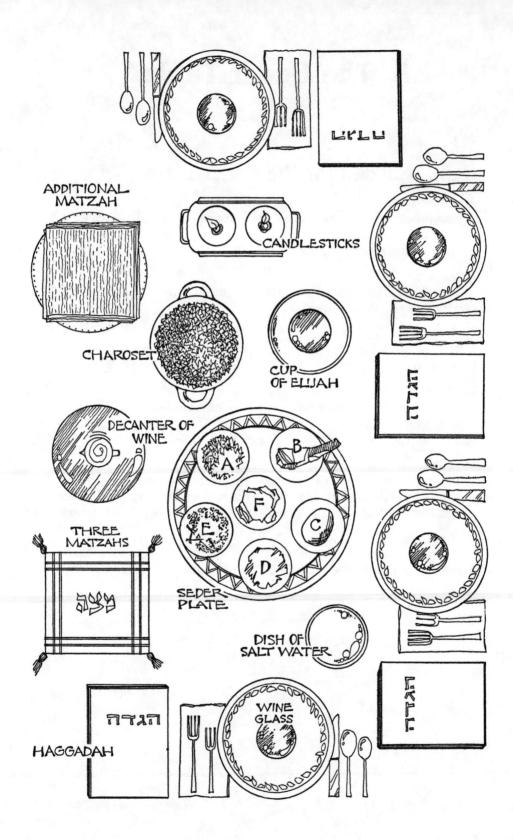

ADDITIONAL MATZAH

CANDLESTICKS

CHAROSET

CUP OF ELIJAH

DECANTER OF WINE

THREE MATZAHS

SEDER PLATE

DISH OF SALT WATER

WINE GLASS

HAGGADAH

הגדה

מצות

נחש

הגדה

Setting the Seder Table

Seder plate

The most important item on the table is the Seder plate, containing the symbolic foods. Seder plates are usually beautifully decrated, often with scenes from the Passover story or with Hebrew inscriptions.

Three matzahs

The ceremonial matzahs are placed, one on top of the other, in a special matzah cover or in a napkin. According to a common interpretation, the matzahs represent the three divisions of the Jewish people; Kohen—priest; Levi—assistants in the Temple; Israelites—people of Israel. Some people add a fourth matzah to represent Jews in the Soviet Union, who are not free to observe Passover.

Additional matzah

Additional matzah is placed on a serving plate, for eating during the main meal.

Haggadahs

The Haggadah is the book that is read cover to cover during the evening. It includes the story, prayers, songs, rituals, and commentary that make up the Seder. Make sure you have one at each place.

Dish of salt water

Part of the Seder ritual is to dip the Karpas (parsley) into salt water, which represents the tears of the Jewish people while in slavery.

Wine glasses

The glasses are filled with the traditional, Kosher for Passover, grape wine.

Decanter of wine

There should be enough wine to pour four cups for each individual. These represent the four divine promises of redemption found in Exodus 6:6-7. You will also need enough wine for serving during the meal.

Cup of Elijah

Fill a beautiful cup with wine and put it in a prominent place on the table to welcome Elijah, the prophet who heralds freedom and redemption.

Charoset

Although charoset goes on the Seder plate, extra charoset is served for making the Hillel sandwich and to eat during the meal. Rabbi Hillel, a great Jewish teacher who lived between 90 B.C.E. and 70 C.E., may have invented this sandwich of charoset and moror (between two pieces of matzah) to represent the bitterness of slavery and the sweetness of freedom.

Candlesticks

The blessing over the candles is recited before the Seder begins.

Pillows

Pillows to lean on are traditionally placed in the chairs, especially in the chair of the leader of the Seder, as a symbol of freedom from slavery.

Food Processor and Microwave

Tips for Using Your Food Processor

You do not have to use a food processor to make or enjoy most of the recipes in this book. Only a few are too cumbersome to make any other way, and a few others will only have the intended texture and flavor if made with a processor. Conventional instructions are included wherever they are applicable. Some recipes do not specify using your processor, but if you do use it to chop, slice, and/or combine ingredients, you can save a great deal of time.

You will get the best results from your processor if you follow the manufacturer's instruction manual. The hints that follow apply to all processors and will help you prepare the recipes in this book regardless of the type of equipment you have.

General

1. When chopping or mixing, use pulse lever or the on-off manually to control the consistency.

2. Arrange even-sized chunks of food around the work bowl and pulse until the desired texture is reached.

3. Generally, you should cut onions and green peppers into quarters, carrots and celery into 2-inch lengths, sticks of butter and 8-ounce packages of cream cheese into 8 pieces, and so on.

4. When combining ingredients, process the firmer ingredients first, then the softer ones (for example, if you were making potato pancakes, you would process the potatoes, then the onions, then the eggs).

5. For thicker slices or a coarse shred, press down firmly on the pusher. Press it lightly for thinner slices or a fine shred.

6. Use your pusher as a "pattern" when cutting food to fit the feed tube.

7. Most feed tubes hold 1 cup. On some models, the pusher also holds 1 cup.

8. Don't overprocess! Stop your machine often and check on your ingredients. This will also give you more uniform pieces.

9. If you want to empty a full work bowl without removing the blade, lift the bowl off carefully, insert your middle finger in the hole under the bowl, gripping the base of the blade tightly against the center. Then tip bowl to empty. This will prevent the blade from dropping out.

Specific Foods

Butter and cream cheese
Use directly from the refrigerator. Cut in chunks to process.

Cheese
Chop parmesan with the metal blade; grate other cheeses. Or, even better, chop any cheese by first cutting into 1-inch cubes and pulsing until desired texture is reached. If you are using the slicing blade or grating blade, use light pressure on the pusher. Softer cheeses will grate better after spending a few minutes in the freezer.

Chocolate
Process until fine so that it will melt faster. One 1-ounce square equals 1/4 cup "grated." (Process several ounces at a time and keep in refrigerator for later use.)

Cream, whipping
Cream whipped with a food processor gets very thick and is wonderful for use as a decoration or filling, but it will not double in volume as it will when whipped with an electric mixer.

Egg whites, beaten
Have at room temperature and process for 7 to 8 seconds. With machine running, add 1 tablespoon water mixed with 1 tablespoon vinegar and process for about 1 1/2 to 2 minutes or until whipped and stiff.

Garlic
Drop through the feed tube with the machine running and process until chopped. Or add to a dip or spread which is already in the work bowl and process until well incorporated.

Herbs, fresh
Dry with a towel and remove all large stems before processing. (These will keep well in the refrigerator.)

Matzah
Three matzahs or 2 cups of matzah farfel processed for 45–60 seconds will make 1 cup of matzah meal.

Meat and poultry, to slice
Arrange on a cookie sheet and freeze for about 40 minutes. You should still be able to penetrate the meat with the tip of a knife. Stack in feed tube and slice against the grain.

Nuts

¼ pound equals 1 cup ground nuts. Process no more than 1½ cups at a time for no longer than 6–8 seconds or you'll have nut butter.

Oil

Add oil with the machine running in order to make a good emulsion in a dip or dressing.

Orange juice, frozen

Reconstitute by processing with 1 cup of water (no more, or you'll have spillage to clean up). Pour into pitcher and add rest of the water called for.

Purees, fruit and vegetable

For smoother purees, process cooked fruits and vegetables separately from their liquids. This is important for making cream soups.

Spinach

To slice, stack the leaves, roll up, and place vertically in the feed tube; use light pressure.

Sugar, fine

Process granulated sugar for 15–20 seconds. Measure after processing.

Sugars, fruit

Add a 1/4-inch piece of any citrus peel to the sugar as you process.

Tomatoes, canned

Drain off the liquid before processing.

Tomatoes, fresh

Before processing, squeeze tomatoes over a strainer or colander to remove juice and seeds. Juice may be substituted for an equal amount of water in your recipe.

Vegetables

Cut small ones in half, larger ones in quarters, before processing. Slice using pressure on the pusher to correspond with texture of vegetables, i.e., medium pressure for carrots and potatoes, light for tomatoes and green peppers. For beautiful slices, cut both ends of vegetables (or fruit) flat and then pack the feed tube tightly so that pieces cannot tilt sideways.

Vegetables, leftover

Puree and use to thicken soups, sauces, or gravies.

Tips for Using Your Microwave

Settings for Cooking

Cooking times vary with each model, depending on oven wattage. A 600–700 watt oven is standard. Foods that retain heat the longest, such as meats, baked potatoes, and casseroles, should be cooked first. Others (breads, rolls, and desserts) only need reheating just before they are served. As the following settings show, different percentages of power are used for cooking in the microwave oven:

High	100%
Reheat	80%
Medium	50%
Low	10%

Cooking Utensils and Coverings

Some utensils shouldn't be used in a microwave oven, especially those made of metal or having a metal trim.

Some utensils don't work well in the microwave oven. A good test of a utensil is to put it in the oven, place one cup of water in it, and turn the oven on high for one minute. If the utensil is cool and water is hot, the utensil is safe; if the utensil is warm and the water is warm, do not use it in the microwave. It may crack or break!

Paper towels: Helps prevent spattering inside the oven and absorbs the moisture from baked products. (Sandwich bread will never get soggy.) For use in other than baked products, paper towels should be securely fastened to prevent inadequate coverage.

Plastic wrap: Holds in heat and steam. To prevent steam buildup, it should be vented by folding back one corner. Use when you do not have a tight-fitting lid.

Wax paper: Good when a light cover is needed, as for a soft boiled egg. It doesn't absorb liquid and the wax won't melt.

Quick and Easy
Microwave Cooking

These times and temperatures are approximate and may vary slightly according to your unit.

Item	Quantity	Power Level	Cooking
Apple, to bake	1	High (9)	4 minutes (uncovered)
Beverage (milk base)	1 cup	Roast (7)	2 minutes
Beverage (water base)	1 cup	High (9)	2 minutes
Brandy, to flame	2 tablespoons	High (9)	15 seconds
Butter, to melt	2 tablespoons	Roast (7)	1 minute
	4 tablespoons	Roast (7)	1½ minutes
	6 tablespoons	Roast (7)	2 minutes
Butter, to soften	1 stick	Low (l)	15–30 seconds
Cheese, to bring to room temp. from refrigerator	½ pound	Medium (5)	45–60 seconds
Baking chocolate, to melt	1 ounce	High (9)	2–3 minutes
	½ ounce	High (9)	45 seconds
Cream cheese, to soften in pkg.	3 ounces	Low (1)	2–2½ minutes
	8 ounces	Low (1)	4–5 minutes
Crumb topping	½ cup crumbs + 4 tablespoons butter	Roast (7)	1½ minutes
Crumb topping with cheese	½ cup crumbs + 4 tablespoons butter + 2 tablespoons grated cheese	Roast (7)	1½ minutes
Egg, to bake	1 large (pierce the yolk)	Medium (5)	30 seconds (soft)

Item	Quantity	Power Level	Cooking
Garlic oil	1 clove minced garlic + 2 tablespoons oil	High (9)	1 minute
Glaze (for pie, tarts, meats, or poultry)	¼ cup preserves	High (9)	2 minutes
Ice cream, to soften	1 quart	Low (1)	5 minutes
Lemon or lime, uncut (for maximum juice)	1 or 2	High (9)	15 seconds
Mushrooms, to saute	1 pound + 1 tablespoon butter or margarine	High (9)	3–4 minutes
Nuts, to brown	¾ cup	High (9)	2–3 minutes (rotate after 1 min.)
Nuts, to saute in melted butter	¾ cup	High (9)	6 minutes (stir twice)
Onion, sliced, to saute	1 onion + 4 tablespoons butter or margarine	High (9)	2 minutes
Orange juice to defrost (remove metal rim)	6-ounce can 12-ounce can	Defrost (4) Defrost (4)	3½ minutes 6 minutes (let stand 2–3 min.)
Potato chips, to freshen	2 cups	Roast (7)	30–45 seconds
Potatoes, boiling	2	High (9)	10–11 minutes (cook in their skins)
Potatoes, baking	2 small	High (9)	7–8 minutes
Tomatoes, to peel	1 small	High (9)	12–15 seconds (let stand 1 min.)

Conversion Table

Ingredient	Passover Substitute
Baking powder, 1 teaspoon	½ teaspoon baking soda + ½ teaspoon cream of tartar
Bread crumbs, ¾ cup	One 12-ounce box crushed soup nuts
Chocolate, 1 ounce	3 tablespoons cocoa + 1 tablespoon shortening (may also use Passover chocolate bar)
Confectioners' sugar, 1 cup	From 1 cup granulated sugar, remove ½ tablespoon and replace with potato starch
Cornstarch	Equal amount of potato starch
Flour	Equal amounts of cake meal and potato starch, sifted together
Flour as sauce thickener (1 tablespoon)	½ tablespoon potato starch or 1 egg yolk
Gelatin, sweetened (non-kosher)* 1 box (3 oz.)	About two 3-ounce boxes Kosher l'Pesach gelatin (same conversion as kosher gelatin)
Gelatin, unflavored (non-kosher)* 1 envelope	About 2 tablespoons Kosher l'Pesach gelatin (same conversion as kosher gelatin)
Graham cracker crumbs, 1 cup	1 cup ground soup nuts or Passover cookies + 1 teaspoon cinnamon
Vanilla extract, 1 teaspoon	The scraped inside of half a vanilla bean, or 2 teaspoons vanilla sugar

*If you keep a kosher kitchen, you will need to buy kosher gelatin at all times, and Kosher l'Pesach gelatin for Passover. This conversion from non-kosher to kosher gelatin will enable you to convert ordinary recipes using gelatin.

illinois world of our flavors south bend indiana the cookery cedar rapids
wa specialties of the house alexandria louisiana kitchen treats cookboo
es to noshes lewiston maine sisterhood cookbook potomac maryland p
nelting pot lexington massa·   ·hought cookbook newton
ok norwood massachus·   ody massachusetts cc
etts in the best of tast·   e happy cooker of te
with temple beth   a used to make f
igan all the recip   o ask saint pau
souri deborah d   o generation
rry hill new je   eating east
son new jers   with love s
le tinton fa   y the spice
ooking? al   onderful
k cookie   york the
ng brook   osher ki
like it cl   ast nor
new yo   great r
york th   it vern
a had   sher c
osher   ester
scars   what
ood ta   d nev
carol   ohi
ount t   nd ol
io in t   nia th
ania th   n per
ia pen   penr
n wynr   south
charles   rolina
e recipe   years
nnial co   oks fall
nchburg   n good
e it parke   sin from
gham alab   eat and en
ste berkele   ills califor
california fr   hat's cookir
flavored with   iego californ
lectable collec   ease! rockvill
d connecticut foc   passover made
earwater florida cle   a measures and tre
ght gainesville florida   alabustas' more favo
it in the kitchen hollyw   s hollywood florida nil
ksonville florida what's coo   ville florida try it you'll like
atellite beach florida our favorite recipes tallahassee florida knishes gefil
georgia golden soup atlanta georgia the happy cooker augusta georgi
ois portal to good cooking great lakes illinois the fort sheridan and great I

Menus
&
Recipes

Menus for Passover

Dairy Menus

Fish Pate with Tomato-Herb
  Sauce*
Macaroni and Cheese,
  Passover Style*
Brussels Sprouts with Mock
  Hollandaise Sauce*
Poached Pears*

Blender Beet Borscht*
Red and White Cole Slaw*
Cheese Blintzes*
Lemon Angel Pie*

Broiled Grapefruit Halves*
Cucumber Salad*
Baked Stuffed Whitefish*
Carrot Puree*
Vegetable Muffins*
Macaroon Delight*

*Indicates recipe in book

Fruit Cup
Fresh Fish Croquettes*
Boiled New Potatoes with
  Sour Cream and Chives*
Vanilla pudding or ice cream
  with Brandy Sauce*

Stewed Tomato Pudding*
Fresh Lake Trout Baked in
  Wine*
Molded Spinach Salad*
Passover Cream Puffs*

Meat Menus

Eggplant Caviar*
Tossed Green Salad
Veal Scallops with Lemon*
Potato Puffs*
Baked Apple Slices*

Tomato Juice
Bibb Lettuce Salad*
Roasted Lamb*
Creamed Spinach*
Sweet Potato Souffle*
Lemon Squares*

Garlic Mushrooms*
Turkey Schnitzel*
Baked Tomatoes with Basil*
Matzah Kugel with White Wine Sauce*
Apple Squares*

Egg Drop Soup*
Meat Loaf*
Spinach Souffle*
Roasted Potatoes*
Passover Lemon Cake Roll*

Sliced Tomatoes and Lettuce
Any left over meat with
    Barbecue Sauce*
Hot Potato Salad Lyonnaise
    Style*
Passover Onion Rolls*
Hazelnut Torte*

*Indicates recipe in book

Menu #1 for the Seder

Serves 12

Hillel Sandwich
(Bitter herbs and charoset* on matzah)

Hard-Cooked Eggs *(with or without salt water)*   Matzah

Egg Drop Soup*

Avocado and Grapefruit Salad with Honey Dressing*

Baked Breast of Chicken*

Roasted Potatoes*   Asparagus with Lemon Sauce*

Passover Sponge Cake*   Red Raspberry Sorbet*

Wine   Tea   Coffee

*Indicates recipe in book

Preparation Timetable

Several days ahead
Make sorbet; place in freezer. Cook the eggs. Make the soup. Make Honey Dressing. Refrigerate. Take out serving platters and serving utensils. Plan how many plates and dishes you will need and make sure you have enough.

Day before
Set Seder table. Make sure you have everything you need for the Seder plate. Bake sponge cake; cover. Peel and section grapefruit. Prepare chicken breasts for baking. Parboil and peel potatoes. Refrigerate grapefruit, chicken, and potatoes.

Day of Seder
Peel the eggs. Make charoset. Prepare Seder plate; cover with plastic wrap. Prepare potatoes for roasting. Make asparagus and lemon sauce, place in serving dish that can be used for reheating. Wash and shred lettuce. Make salt water (by heating a small amount of

water with salt until salt dissolves). Refrigerate eggs, charoset, potatoes, asparagus and sauce, and lettuce. Finish setting table and arrange flowers.

One hour before your Seder begins
Place hard-cooked eggs in small bowls for serving. Slice cake and place on platter; cover with plastic wrap. Peel avocado and make up salad plates. Dilute salt water in pitcher. Place the plate of three matzahs on the table in addition to matzah for the meal. Fill wine cups. Brew tea and make coffee.

One hour before serving the main meal
Turn on oven 350° F, and place chicken in oven. Heat soup over low heat. After chicken has cooked about 30 minutes, place potatoes in oven.

When ready to serve the main meal
Reheat the asparagus. Remove sorbet from freezer and place in refrigerator.

Recipes

Charoset

1 cup nuts (walnuts, pecans, almonds, or all three)
5 apples, peeled and cored
1 teaspoon grated lemon peel
3 tablespoons sweet red wine, or more to taste
1½ tablespoon sugar
1 tablespoon cinnamon
Dash of ground ginger

Processor

Insert metal blade, and chop the nuts with 1 or 2 pulses. Cut apples into 1-inch pieces and add to work bowl with the remaining ingredients. Pulse several times, until everything is chopped medium-fine. Scrape sides of bowl with rubber spatula and make sure nothing gets lodged on the blade. Adjust seasonings. Cover and refrigerate.

Conventional

Follow processor instructions, chopping nuts and apples with a sharp knife or in a chopping bowl. Makes about 2 cups.

Egg Drop Soup

12 cups chicken broth or
 Chicken Soup (see
 recipe)
5 eggs, beaten

You may want to add some minced cooked chicken for flavor or a little chopped parsley for color.

1. Heat chicken broth until it comes to a boil.
2. Pour beaten eggs into the broth and stir with a wire whisk until the eggs are set.

Serves 12

Avocado and Grapefruit Salad

4 large avocados
4 large grapefruit
1 head iceberg lettuce,
 shredded
Honey Dressing (recipe
 follows)

This simple salad may be prepared earlier in the day by slicing the avocados and marinating them in lemon juice or grapefruit juice. I prefer pink grapefruit as it is not quite as bitter.

1. Peel avocados and cut into lengthwise slices.
2. Peel grapefruit and cut into segments.
3. Place some lettuce on each plate. Arrange avocado and grapefruit on the lettuce and pour Honey Dressing over the top.

Serves 10 to 12

Honey Dressing

1 cup white vinegar
½ cup dry red wine
½ cup sugar
6 tablespoons honey

This dressing will keep for several weeks in the pantry; it does not need to be refrigerated.

Combine all ingredients and mix with food processor for 5 seconds (using the metal blade), or shake well in a jar. Makes 2 cups.

Baked Breast of Chicken

4 whole chicken breasts,
  boned
1 cup soup nut crumbs
1 teaspoon ground ginger
1 teaspoon garlic powder
½ teaspoon salt
¼ teaspoon white pepper
2 eggs, well beaten
1 cup apricot preserves
½ cup white wine
2 tablespoons pareve
  margarine

This may be made a day ahead and reheated.

1. Preheat oven to 350°F. Cut chicken breasts in half. Rinse with cold water and dry well with paper towels.

2. Combine soup nut crumbs, ginger, garlic powder, salt, and pepper in a shallow dish.

3. Dip each chicken part in beaten egg, then in crumb mixture. Arrange in a single layer in a baking pan.

4. Combine preserves, wine, and margarine. Microwave on high setting for 5 minutes, or bring to a boil in a small saucepan. Pour over the chicken breasts and bake for 1 hour.

Serves 6; double recipe to serve 12

Roasted Potatoes

8 medium potatoes
  (about 2 pounds)
1 cup ketchup
Salt and pepper to taste

These are pretty and tasty. If you are making a pot roast, you may also bake the potatoes with some of the gravy from the roast.

1. Preheat oven to 350°F.

2. Parboil the potatoes in ½ cup water for 10 minutes. Drain, peel, and cut each one into 4 equal pieces. Roll each piece in ketchup until well coated. Season with salt and pepper.

3. Bake, uncovered, for 30 minutes or until a hard golden brown crust forms on the potatoes.

Serves 12

Asparagus with Lemon Sauce

1 pound fresh asparagus
¼ teaspoon salt
Lemon Sauce (recipe
   follows)

Microwave

1. Wash asparagus and bend each stalk gently until tough end snaps off. Peel off outer skin below the tip with a vegetable peeler.

2. Add salt to ¼ cup water in a 12″ x 8″ microwave-safe baking dish. Arrange asparagus with tips toward the center. Cover with vented plastic wrap and cook on high setting for 4 minutes.

3. Rotate the asparagus so that spears along the outer edges are in the center, and vice versa. Cover again and cook on high for 3 to 5 minutes or until asparagus is tender-crisp. Let stand covered for 3 minutes.

4. While asparagus is cooking, make the Lemon Sauce.

Conventional

In step 2, place asparagus in a small amount of boiling, salted water (tie asparagus with white string and stand upright in a tall pot, or place flat in a large skillet). Cover, and cook for 6 minutes or until tender.

Serves 6; double recipe to serve 12

Lemon Sauce

1 tablespoon potato
   starch
4 tablespoons pareve
   margarine
Juice and grated peel of 1
   large lemon

1. In a small saucepan, mix potato starch with 1 tablespoon cold water. Add margarine and cook over medium heat, stirring until it begins to thicken. Gradually stir in 1 cup hot water.

2. Add lemon juice and grated peel, and stir until well blended. Makes 1½ cups.

Passover Sponge Cake

10 eggs, room
   temperature
⅓ cup potato starch
⅓ cup matzah cake meal
1 heaping cup sugar
Juice and grated peel of 2
   lemons

Every Passover, my friend Sylvia would bring me this sponge cake for my Seder meal, and on Rosh Hashanah I would take her my strudel. We kept this tradition for many years.

1. Separate the eggs about 1 hour before beginning cake. Place whites in large bowl of electric mixer and yolks in the smaller bowl.

2. Preheat oven to 350°F. Sift together potato starch and cake meal.

3. Beat egg whites until frothy. Turn mixer to high speed and add the sugar, one tablespoon at a time. (I add 1 tablespoon, then count to 10 and add the next one, until all the sugar is added.) It is important to do this slowly so that you beat enough air into the whites. This is what makes the cake high.

4. Beat the egg yolks with the lemon juice and peel until thickened. Fold into beaten egg whites.

5. Using a rubber spatula, fold the dry ingredients into the egg white mixture.

6. Pour the batter into an ungreased 10-inch tube pan with removable bottom (or angel-food cake pan) and bake in the middle rack of the pre-heated oven for 45 to 60 minutes, or until top begins to crack just a little.

7. Remove from oven and invert pan to cool. If pan does not have legs, invert over neck of a bottle. (The cake won't fall out!) Cool for 1 hour. Remove from pan.

Serves 12 to 14.

Note: This cake may be iced with a lemon glaze, but I like it plain.

Red Raspberry Sorbet

⅔ cup sugar
2 cups crushed fresh strawberries (or 10-oz. package frozen raspberries)
½ cup red raspberry syrup
Grated peel of 1 orange
1 egg white (may substitute 1 cup heavy cream with a dairy meal)

This is a French sherbet. Quite easy and elegant! It will keep up to 2 weeks in the freezer.

Processor

1. Combine sugar with ⅔ cup water in a saucepan and cook over medium heat until sugar dissolves. (Don't let it come to boil.) Let cool.

2. Insert metal blade, and process strawberries, raspberry syrup, and grated orange peel for 1 minute. Add cooled syrup and process until mixture is smooth. Pour into metal container and freeze.

3. Several hours before serving, remove from freezer. Break up to fit into work bowl. Process with metal blade, adding egg white or cream through feed tube while machine is running.

4. Return to metal bowl, cover, and refreeze. Let soften a little before serving.

Serves 6 to 8; double recipe for 12

Menu #2 for the Seder

Serves 8

Hillel Sandwich
(Bitter herbs and charoset* on matzah)

Hard-Cooked Eggs *(with or without salt water)*   Matzah

Gefilte Fish Mousse with Horseradish Sauce*

Roast Pickled Tongue*

Tossed Salad   Eggplant Fritters*

Brussels Sprouts with Mock Hollandaise Sauce*

Passover Lemon Cake Roll*

Wine   Tea   Coffee

*Indicates recipe in book

Preparation Timetable

Several days ahead
Cook the eggs. Make eggplant fritters and place in freezer. Prepare tongue (do not bake) and make gefilte fish mousse. Refrigerate eggs, tongue, and mousse. Take out serving platters and serving utensils. Plan how many plates and dishes you will need and make sure you have enough.

Day before
Set Seder table. Make sure you have everything you need for the Seder plate. Make lemon roll (but not meringue), brussels sprouts, mock hollandaise sauce, and horseradish sauce; refrigerate.

Day of Seder
Peel the eggs. Unmold the mousse. Make charoset. Prepare Seder plate and cover with plastic wrap. Make meringue and finish lemon roll. Wash and tear up salad greens and place in large bowl with dressing in bottom. Slice tongue; place in casserole with sauce. Make

salt water (by heating a small amount of water with salt until salt dissolves). Refrigerate eggs, mousse, charoset, lemon cake roll, salad, tongue, and salt water. Finish setting table and arrange flowers. Two or three hours before the Seder, remove fritters from freezer and place on cookie sheets.

One hour before serving the main meal
Place tongue in oven. Place hard-cooked eggs in small bowls for individual servings. Pour wine in cups. Remove brussels sprouts and sauce from refrigerator and prepare for heating in oven or microwave. Place the plate of three matzahs on the table in addition to matzah for the meal. Dilute salt water in a pitcher. Pour wine in cups. Brew tea and make coffee.

When ready to serve the main meal
Turn on oven to 325° F. As soon as tongue is heated, turn oven to 400° and heat the fritters. Toss salad. Reheat brussels sprouts and hollandaise.

Recipes

Gefilte Fish Mousse

2 boxes (3 oz. each)
  unflavored kosher
  gelatin*
½ cup white wine
24-ounce jar gefilte fish,
  drained (save broth)
½ cup mayonnaise
1 tablespoon chopped
  chives
½ teaspoon vinegar
Horseradish Sauce
  (recipe follows) or
  horseradish

Processor

1. Lightly grease a 1½ quart mold.

2. Soften gelatin in wine. Add fish broth and microwave on high setting for 2 minutes, or heat on top of range until gelatin dissolves. Set aside.

3. Insert metal blade. Place mayonnaise and gelatin mixture in work bowl and blend with 1 or 2 pulses. Add gefilte fish, 4 pieces at a time, and pulse 2 or 3 times until blended into the mixture. Add chives and vinegar; pulse to incorporate. Pour into mold and chill well.

4. Unmold and slice. Serve with horseradish or Horseradish Sauce.

Serves 8

*Kosher gelatin gels differently from non-kosher gelatin. See conversion table.

Horseradish Sauce

½ cup mayonnaise
½ cup non-dairy creamer
3 tablespoons lemon juice
2 ½ tablespoons red or
  white horseradish
⅛ teaspoon ground
  cumin seed
Dash of red pepper

Combine all ingredients and beat with processor (metal blade), electric mixer, or wire whisk until well blended. Makes about 1 cup.

Roast Pickled Tongue

1 pickled beef tongue, 2
  pounds or less
1 tart apple (Granny
  Smith or McIntosh)
1 stalk celery with leaves
1 bay leaf
6 whole peppercorns
8-ounce can tomato sauce
  (see conversion table)
½ cup ketchup
½ pound roasted brisket,
  sliced (optional)

The addition of the brisket adds flavor. I use the second cut.

1. Preheat oven to 325° F.

2. Place tongue in a 4-quart pot. Add just enough cold water to cover. Place over high heat and bring to a boil. Drain off water. Repeat this procedure, draining off water again.

3. Cut up apple and celery, and add to pot with bay leaf and peppercorns. Add cold water to cover. Bring to a boil, then cover and simmer 50 minutes per pound, or until tender.

4. When tender, plunge tongue into cold water to cool. Skin immediately. (It is much harder to skin if you let it get cold first.) Trim tongue, removing roots, small bones, and gristle.

5. Slice on the diagonal. Place the slices in an 8″ x 11″ baking dish. Combine the tomato sauce and ketchup with ½ cup hot water and pour over the tongue. Cover with brisket slices. (The dish may be prepared up to this point, refrigerated, and finished later.)

6. Place in oven and roast, uncovered, 15 to 20 minutes, or until the tomato sauce has thickened.

Serves 8

Eggplant Fritters

1 small eggplant, peeled
1 small onion, cut in half
1 egg, beaten
2 tablespoons ketchup
½ teaspoon salt
Dash of white pepper
½ cup matzah cake meal
  (approx.)
½ to ¾ cup oil for frying

Processor

1. Cut eggplant into cubes. Place in saucepan with ¼ cup water and bring to a boil. Cover and simmer 10 to 15 minutes until tender. Drain.

2. Insert metal blade. Mince onion with several pulses. Add eggplant to work bowl. Pulse 3 times, scraping sides of bowl between pulses. Add beaten egg, tomato sauce, salt, and pepper. Add matzah cake meal, 1 tablespoon at a time. (Depending on the size of the eggplant, you may need to add a little more or less cake meal to make the batter the right consistency to hold together.) Mix well, stopping to scrape the sides of bowl.

3. Heat oil in frying pan to about 360° F. Drop batter by tablespoons into the oil. Fry until brown, about 2 to 3 minutes on each side. Turn the pancakes only once, or they will get soggy. Drain on absorbent towels and serve immediately.* Serve with sour cream for a dairy meal.

Conventional

In step 2, grate the onion and mash the eggplant with a fork or potato masher until smooth. Proceed to step 4.

Makes 12 to 14

*If you are making these ahead, do not drain. Arrange on a cookie sheet in a single layer and place in freezer for 2 hours. Then remove from cookie sheet and place in airtight container or plastic bag. When ready to serve, preheat oven to 400° F, lay pancakes on cookie sheet in single layer, and heat for 10 minutes.

Brussels Sprouts with Mock Hollandaise Sauce

1 to 1½ pounds brussels
  sprouts
⅛ teaspoon ground
  nutmeg
Salt and pepper to taste
Mock Hollandaise Sauce
  (recipe follows)

Microwave

1. Pull off wilted leaves and trim bottom of each sprout. Soak for about 10 minutes in cold water to which a little salt has been added. Remove and wash with cold water. Cut an X in each stem end.

2. Place in a 2-quart microwave safe baking dish, add ¼ cup water, and cover with vented plastic wrap. Microwave on high setting 10 to 12 minutes.

3. Season with nutmeg, salt, and pepper. Pour Mock Hollandaise Sauce over sprouts.

Conventional

In step 2, place brussels sprouts in a saucepan with ¼ cup boiling, salted water, cover, and simmer about 15 minutes until tender.

Mock Hollandaise Sauce

1 cup mayonnaise
¼ cup non-dairy creamer
Juice of 1 lemon (about
  ⅓ cup)
½ teaspoon sugar
Dash of red pepper

1. Combine all ingredients in a blender or food processor (using metal blade) for 30 seconds, or beat with wire whisk.

2. Heat in small saucepan over hot water, or microwave in a covered microwave-safe container for 1 minute on high setting. Makes about 1½ cups.

DIAGRAM FOR CAKE ROLL

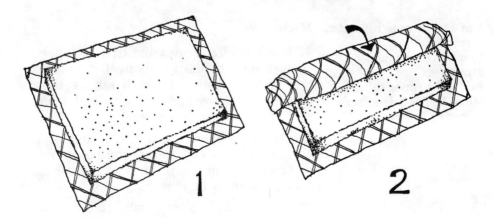

1

2

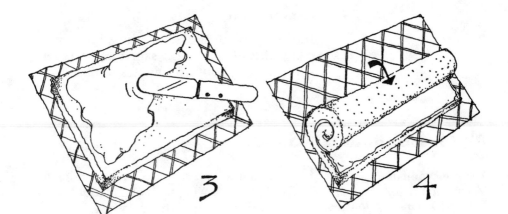

3

4

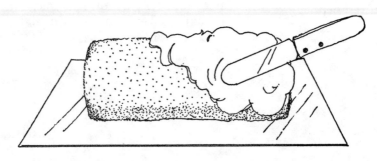

5

Passover Lemon Cake Roll

4 eggs, separated
⅔ cup granulated sugar (divided)
1 tablespoon lemon juice
½ teaspoon grated lemon peel
⅓ cup potato starch
⅓ cup matzah cake meal
¼ teaspoon salt
⅓ cup confectioners' sugar (see conversion table)
Lemon Filling (recipe follows)
Meringue (recipe follows)

1. Preheat oven to 350° F. Grease a 10 x 15 jelly roll pan. Cover with wax paper; grease the paper.

2. Beat the egg whites in large bowl of electric mixer until soft peaks form (tips will curl over). Gradually add ⅓ cup granulated sugar, beating until stiff peaks form (tips will stand straight up).

3. In small bowl of mixer, beat egg yolks at high speed until thick and lemon-colored (about 5 minutes). Gradually add ⅓ cup granulated sugar, beating constantly. Stir in lemon juice and grated peel. Gently fold yolk mixture into the whites.

4. Sift together potato starch, matzah cake meal, and salt. Gently fold, half at a time, into egg mixture until just blended.

5. Spread batter evenly in pan and bake 15 minutes, or until cake tests done. (Wooden toothpick inserted in center of cake will come out clean.)

6. Remove from oven and let cool for 5 minutes in pan. Turn out onto towel or aluminum foil that has been sprinkled generously with confectioners' sugar. Roll up cake and towel together from the long end. Let cool completely. Refrigerate (rolled up) while you prepare the filling.

7. Unroll cake and spread evenly with the filling. Roll up and place on ungreased cookie sheet, seam side down.

8. Ice evenly over top and sides with meringue. Brown in oven for 10 minutes at 350° F; turn off oven and allow cake to remain for 5 more minutes. Place in refrigerator until serving time.

Serves 10

Lemon Filling

¾ cup sugar
2 tablespoons potato
  starch
Dash of salt
2 egg yolks, slightly
  beaten
Grated peel of 1 lemon
3 tablespoons lemon juice
1 tablespoon pareve
  margarine

1. Combine sugar, potato starch, and salt in a medium saucepan.

2. Stir in egg yolks, grated lemon peel, lemon juice, and ¾ cup water. Cook and stir over medium heat until bubbly. Boil 1 minute only!

3. Remove from heat and stir in margarine. Then let cool without stirring. When filling is cool, assemble cake roll.

Fills 1 cake roll or 10 to 12 puffs

Meringue

1 teaspoon potato starch
¼ cup plus 1 tablespoon
  granulated sugar
2 egg whites
1 teaspoon vanilla (see
  conversion table)

1. In a 1-quart saucepan, combine potato starch and 1 tablespoon sugar with ¼ cup water. Bring to a boil, then lower heat and simmer until thick. Cool.

2. Place egg whites in small bowl of electric mixer. Beat until soft peaks form, then add ¼ cup sugar, 1 teaspoon at a time, potato starch mixture, and vanilla.

3. Spread evenly over cake. Brown for 10 minutes in a 350° F oven; turn off oven and allow to remain for 5 minutes. Refrigerate.

Appetizers & First Courses

Salmon Pate

1 small onion, cut in half
¼ cup fresh parsley
2 cups cooked salmon
1 stick (½ cup) butter or
   margarine (may
   substitute 3 oz. cream
   cheese for ½ stick)
½ cup pecans
1 tablespoon lemon juice
1 teaspoon horseradish
1 teaspoon salt

The flavor and texture will be different if this pate is not made with a food processor.

Processor

1. Insert metal blade. With machine running, drop onion and parsley through the feed tube. Add salmon to the work bowl and process for 15 seconds. Scrape work bowl, add remaining ingredients, and process 30 seconds. Push down with scraper and process for 30 seconds more.

2. Chill for several hours. Serve with matzah or Miniature Passover Rolls.

Makes about 3 cups; serves 8 to 10

Fish Pate with Tomato-Herb Sauce

3 bunches watercress
(leaves only)
1 tablespoon butter or
margarine
2 tablespoons sliced
shallots
1 ½ pounds salmon or
sole fillets cut into
1-inch cubes (for more
color, use 1 lb. salmon
and ½ lb. sole)
1 ½ cups whipping
cream
2 eggs
½ teaspoon plus 2
pinches of salt
2 dashes of white pepper
2 pinches of nutmeg
3 tablespoons lemon juice
Tomato-Herb Sauce
(recipe follows)

Processor

1. Cook the watercress in the microwave with ¼ cup water, covered, for 1 minute, or on the range in large pot of boiling water. Drain in colander, rinse in cold water, and drain well, pressing out excess water.

2. Melt the butter in a skillet, add shallots, and saute until translucent.

3. Preheat oven to 400° F. Oil a loaf pan (8 ½ x 4 ½ x 2 ½).

4. Insert metal blade. Chop 1 pound of fish with half the shallots until smooth. Add 1 cup cream, 1 egg, ½ teaspoon salt, dash of pepper, and nutmeg. Process until well combined. Remove 2 cups of mixture from work bowl and spread evenly in loaf pan.

5. Add watercress to remaining fish mixture and process until watercress is pureed. Spread over fish layer in loaf pan.

6. Place remaining fish in work bowl with remaining shallots. Process until smooth. Add ½ cup cream, 1 egg, 2 pinches of salt, dash of pepper, and the lemon juice. Process until well combined. Scrape bowl as necessary. Spread evenly over watercress layer.

7. Bake 25 minutes or until knife inserted in center comes out clean. Cool on wire rack about 30 minutes, then cover and refrigerate until chilled.

8. When ready to serve, run knife around inside of pan and invert onto a platter. Slice pate ½ to ¾ inches thick and serve with Tomato-Herb Sauce.

Serves 8 to 10

Tomato-Herb Sauce

16-ounce can whole
  tomatoes, drained and
  seeded
1 cup sour cream
¼ cup fresh parsley
  leaves
1 teaspoon basil
1 teaspoon tarragon
½ teaspoon sugar
½ teaspoon salt
2 dashes red pepper
Dash of white pepper

Mix all ingredients until smooth in blender or food processor (with metal blade). Refrigerate. Makes about 1¾ cups.

Fish Spread

2 pounds cooked fish
  fillets (haddock,
  whitefish, sole), cut in
  2-inch cubes
1 small yellow onion, cut
  in half
½ cup mayonnaise
½ cup sour cream
2 tablespoons lemon juice
1 tablespoon horseradish

Processor

1. Insert metal blade. Chop fish with 3 or 4 pulses. Add onion and pulse 3 or 4 times, scraping down sides of bowl as necessary. Add remaining ingredients, and process for 10 seconds or until fish is of spreading consistency.

2. Grease a 4-cup mold with mayonnaise or oil and fill with fish mixture. Refrigerate for several hours or overnight. Unmold onto lettuce. Serve with fresh vegetables or matzahs.

Conventional

Use a grinder to chop fish and onions. Fold in remaining ingredients and proceed to step 2.

Makes about 1 quart; serves 10 to 12

Gefilte Fish Mousse with Horseradish Sauce

See Seder Menu # 2 for recipe.

Easy Chopped Herring

8-ounce jar pickled
  herring in wine sauce
1 matzah
1 medium tart apple,
  peeled, cored, and cut
  into quarters
1 medium onion, cut into
  quarters
1 teaspoon sugar
Salt and pepper to taste
3 hard-cooked eggs, cut
  in half

*The mixture has better flavor and consistency
when prepared with a food processor. It may be
made a day or two ahead.*

Processor

1. Drain liquid from herring; do not discard.
   Break up matzah and put into herring
   liquid.

2. Insert metal blade. Chop herring, apple,
   onion, and soaked matzah with 2 or 3
   pulses. Add sugar, salt, and pepper. Pulse
   4 or 5 times, scraping down the sides
   between pulses, until mixture is chopped
   to a medium consistency. Remove to a
   bowl.

3. Place eggs in work bowl and pulse 3 or 4
   times to chop. Fold into the herring mixture. Transfer to serving dish or an oiled
   1-quart mold. Refrigerate for several hours.

Serves 6 to 8

Chopped Liver Pate

1 pound chicken livers
1 large onion, cut in
    quarters
2 tablespoons chicken fat
2 hard-cooked eggs, cut
    in half
2 tablespoons mayonnaise
Salt and pepper to taste

Processor

1. Soak the chicken livers in cold salt water for 2 hours. Rinse in cold water and drain on paper towels. Broil the livers.

2. Insert metal blade. With machine running, drop onion through the feed tube.

3. Saute onion in chicken fat in a skillet. Add the broiled livers and saute to blend flavors.

4. Place liver and onions in work bowl and pulse 2 or 3 times, scraping bowl as necessary. Add hard-cooked eggs and mayonnaise. Pulse 2 or 3 times. Process for 10 seconds, scraping sides of bowl as necessary. Season with salt and pepper.

Conventional

In step 2, grate or chop onion. In step 4, put livers, onions, and eggs twice through a grinder.

Makes about 2 cups

Eggplant Caviar

1 small eggplant (about 1
lb.), unpeeled
1 onion
1 green pepper
½ pound fresh
mushrooms
2 cloves garlic
⅓ cup oil
6-ounce can tomato sauce
(see conversion table)
½ cup chopped green
olives
3 tablespoons pine nuts
2 tablespoons ketchup
2 tablespoons vinegar
1 ½ teaspoons sugar
Salt and pepper to taste

Processor

1. Cut eggplant into 1-inch cubes. Cut onion
   and green pepper into quarters. Slice
   mushrooms in half.

2. Insert metal blade. With machine running, drop garlic cloves through feed tube.
   Add eggplant, onion, green pepper, mushrooms, and oil. Chop with several pulses,
   scraping down between pulses until all
   vegetables are chopped fine.

3. Remove to a 1-quart saucepan; cover and
   simmer for 10 minutes.

4. While vegetables are cooking, place tomato
   sauce, olives, pine nuts, ketchup, vinegar,
   and sugar in the work bowl with ¼ cup
   water and combine with 2 pulses. Add to
   vegetables. Season with salt and pepper.
   Cover and simmer for 30 minutes. Chill
   well before serving.

Serves 6 to 8

Marinated Mushrooms

1 pound fresh
mushrooms
½ cup oil
4 tablespoons lemon juice
2 tablespoons vinegar
1 teaspoon parsley
½ teaspoon sugar
Salt and pepper to taste

Processor

1. Insert slicing blade. Place mushrooms in
   feed tube and slice. Remove to a large
   bowl.

2. Change to metal blade. Place remaining
   ingredients in work bowl and process for
   15 seconds until well mixed.

3. Pour over sliced mushrooms and toss well.
   Marinate for several hours before serving.

Conventional

Slice mushroom with a sharp knife. Chop
parsley; use a wire whisk to combine parsley
and remaining ingredients. Proceed to step 3.

Serves 4

Garlic Mushrooms

1 small onion, cut in half
3 cloves garlic
1 pound fresh
   mushrooms
½ cup oil
¼ cup butter or
   margarine
½ cup white wine
1 teaspoon basil
Salt and pepper to taste

Serve these on a lettuce leaf or on small matzah puffs.

Processor

1. Insert metal blade. Drop onion and garlic through feed tube with machine running. Process 5 seconds.

2. Change to slicing blade. Stack mushrooms on their sides in the feed tube and slice, using light pressure.

3. Heat oil and butter in a heavy skillet. Saute mushroom mixture about 5 minutes. Add wine and basil; cook on high heat for 2 minutes. Season with salt and pepper. Let cool, then refrigerate several hours or overnight.

Conventional

Finely chop garlic and onion with a sharp knife. Slice mushrooms. Proceed to step 3.

Serves 6 to 8

Frosted Nuts

2 ½ cups walnut or
   pecan halves
2 egg whites
¼ cup confectioners'
   sugar (see conversion
   table)
¼ teaspoon ginger
¼ teaspoon cinnamon

These are great with drinks before dinner.

1. Spread nuts in a single layer in a jelly roll pan. Bake in a 350° F oven for 10 minutes, stirring occasionally. Cool to room temperature.

2. Turn oven to 250°.

3. With electric mixer, beat egg whites, sugar, and 2 tablespoons of water until egg whites form stiff peaks. Fold in ginger and cinnamon.

4. Fold into toasted nuts until nuts are evenly coated. Return to pan and bake for 15 minutes or until exteriors are dry and crusty. Store in airtight containers.

Cabbage Pirogen

1 recipe Miniature
   Passover Rolls, split in
   half (see recipe)
2 ½ pounds cabbage
5 hard-cooked eggs, cut
   in half
3 tablespoons butter
2 teaspoons salt, or to
   taste
Dash of white pepper

Processor

1. Insert grater blade. Cut cabbage to fit the feed tube, and grate. Place grated cabbage in a colander, pour on about 2 cups boiling water, then rinse with cold water. Drain well, and squeeze by handfuls to remove remaining water.

2. Change to metal blade. Place eggs in work bowl and chop with 3 to 5 pulses, scraping bowl as needed.

3. Heat the butter in a large skillet. Saute cabbage until soft. Add chopped egg, season with salt and pepper, and saute for 1 or 2 minutes.

4. Fill each roll with 1 tablespoon of mixture, and serve warm.

Conventional

Grate the cabbage and chop the eggs. Proceed to step 3.

Makes about 36

Miniature Potato Pancakes

3 medium potatoes,
  peeled
1 small onion
1 large egg
1 tablespoon matzo cake
  meal
¼ teaspoon salt
Dash of white pepper
½ cup oil for frying

Processor

1. Insert grater blade. Cut potatoes to fit the feed tube, and grate with very light pressure. Place in a colander and rinse under cold water to remove the starch.

2. Change to metal blade. Return 1 cup of the grated potatoes to the work bowl and process with 2 or 3 pulses. Stir into grated potatoes.

3. Place remaining ingredients in work bowl and process for 15 seconds. Stir into grated potatoes.

4. Heat oil in frying pan to about 360° F. Drop batter by teaspoons into the oil. Fry until brown. Turn the pancakes only once, or they will get soggy. Drain on absorbent towels and serve immediately.* Serve with sour cream or applesauce.

Conventional

Grate the potatoes and onion. Rinse as in step 1. Combine remaining ingredients. Proceed to step 3.

Makes about 24

*If you are making these ahead, do not drain. Arrange on a cookie sheet in a single layer and place in freezer for 2 hours. Then remove from cookie sheet and place in airtight container or plastic bag. When ready to serve, preheat oven to 400° F, lay pancakes on cookie sheet in single layer, and heat for 10 minutes.

Egg Salad Mold

¼ small onion
12 hard-cooked eggs, cut
    in half
½ cup mayonnaise
¼ cup sour cream
Dash of red pepper
Salt and pepper to taste

Processor

1. Insert metal blade. With machine running, drop the onion through the feed tube. Add 6 eggs to work bowl and pulse 3 times until chopped. Repeat with remaining 6 eggs. Scrape down sides of the bowl as necessary.

2. Add mayonnaise, sour cream, and red pepper. Pulse 4 to 6 times, until you obtain desired texture. Scrape down sides of bowl as necessary. Season with salt and pepper.

3. Oil a 4-cup ring mold and fill with the egg salad. Refrigerate.

Conventional

Rice the eggs, using a food mill or grater. Mince the onion and combine onions and remaining ingredients with the eggs. Proceed to step 3.

Serves 12

Broiled Grapefruit Halves

3 whole pink or white
    grapefruit, cut in half
¼ cup honey
¼ cup orange marmalade
Dash of powdered ginger

1. Turn on broiler. Loosen grapefruit segments with grapefruit knife. Place halves in muffin tin or pan with sides.

2. Combine honey, marmalade, and ginger and brush over top of each grapefruit half.

3. Place 3 inches from the heat and broil for 1 minute, or until tops begin to turn golden brown. Serve warm.

Serves 6

Egg Molds with Chopped Olives

8 hard-cooked eggs, cut
  in half
4 tablespoons mayonnaise
3 to 5 drops onion juice
Salt and pepper to taste
1 cup chopped green
  olives

Processor

1. Insert metal blade. Chop eggs with 3
   pulses. Add mayonnaise and onion juice.
   Pulse 3 or 4 times until you obtain a
   smooth, but not pureed, texture. Scrape
   down sides of the bowl as necessary. Season with salt and pepper.

2. Oil small custard cups or individual souffle dishes and fill with egg mixture. Refrigerate.

3. When ready to serve, run the tip of a
   sharp knife around the molds and unmold
   onto lettuce leaves. With the back of a
   teaspoon, make a depression in the middle
   of each mold and fill with chopped olives.

Conventional

Use a grater or food mill to rice the eggs. Mix
in remaining ingredients and proceed to
step 2.

Serves 8

Cheese Puffs

1 recipe Miniature
  Passover Rolls (see
  recipe)
1 cup mayonnaise
5 tablespoons grated
  parmesan cheese
3 teaspoons horseradish
1 egg white

1. Split rolls, and toast them in a preheated
   broiler.

2. Combine mayonnaise, cheese, and horseradish. Beat egg white until stiff; fold into
   cheese mixture.

3. Drop ½ teaspoon of mixture on top of
   each roll. Broil 2 or 3 minutes.

Makes about 36

Sephardic Charoset

½ cup grated coconut
½ cup ground walnuts
¼ cup sugar
2 teaspoons cinnamon
1 cup raisins
1 cup dried apricots
½ cup dried apples
½ cup dried prunes
½ cup dried pears
12-ounce jar cherry
   preserves
⅓ cup Malaga wine

Processor

1. Insert metal blade. Combine coconut, walnuts, sugar, and cinnamon with 2 or 3 pulses. Add dried fruits and chop with 3 or 4 pulses, until mixture is in medium-size pieces.

2. Place in a 4-quart pot, adding water to cover. Simmer uncovered, stirring occasionally with a wooden spoon, for approximately 1 hour. When mixture begins to thicken and come together, stir in cherry preserves. Remove from heat, add wine, and let cool.

Conventional

Mix coconut, walnuts, sugar, and cinnamon together. Chop dried fruits with a grinder or chopping bowl. Proceed to step 2.

Makes about 3 cups

Charoset

See Seder Menu #1 for recipe.

"Bread"

Passover Rolls

½ cup oil
1 cup water
1 cup matzah meal
1 tablespoon sugar
1 teaspoon salt
4 large eggs

Processor

1. Place oil and water in a saucepan and bring to a boil. Remove pan from heat. Combine the matzah meal, sugar, and salt and add all at once. Beat well with a wooden spoon.

2. Preheat oven to 350° F.

3. Insert metal blade. Put matzah meal mixture into work bowl. With machine running, add eggs through feed tube. Process until a ball is formed. Remove.

4. Oil your hands and shape the dough into 12 small balls. Place on ungreased cookie sheet about 2 inches apart. Bake 50 to 60 minutes.

Conventional

In step 3, beat the eggs into the matzah-meal mixture one at a time, by hand or with electric mixer. Proceed to step 4.

Makes 12

Sweet Rolls (variation)

In step 3 of Passover Rolls recipe, add ¼ cup sugar and 1 tablespoon cinnamon with the eggs, then fold in ½ cup raisins.

Passover Onion Rolls

1 small onion, cut in half
1 tablespoon chicken fat
½ cup oil
1 cup water
1 cup matzah meal
1 ½ teaspoons salt
4 large eggs
1 egg for egg wash
    (optional)
½ teaspoon salt for egg
    wash (optional)

These may be split and used for sandwiches or as a base for tuna, chicken, or egg salads. The dough can be made ahead and refrigerated overnight.

Processor

1. Preheat oven to 350° F. Grease a cookie sheet, and fill a small bowl with cold water.

2. Insert metal blade. With machine running, drop onion into the feed tube and process until minced.

3. Heat chicken fat in small skillet. Saute onions until golden brown. Set aside.

4. Bring oil and water to a boil in a 2-quart saucepan. Remove from heat and add matzah meal and salt all at once. Mix well with wooden spoon.

5. Place in work bowl. Add 2 eggs and pulse until well mixed (about 3 seconds). Add remaining 2 eggs and the onions. Pulse until well mixed. Remove to a mixing bowl.

6. Shape into 2-inch rolls and place about 2 inches apart on the cookie sheet, dipping your hands in the water to avoid sticking.

7. Combine egg and salt for egg wash and brush tops of rolls. Bake 50 to 60 minutes or until golden brown. Cool for several minutes before removing from cookie sheet.

Conventional

In step 2, mince onion with a sharp knife. In step 5, use electric mixer.

Makes 12

Garlic Bread

½ cup plus 2 tablespoons
  oil
1 cup water
1 cup matzah meal
1 teaspoon salt
1 teaspoon chopped fresh
  basil
4 large eggs
2 cloves garlic

Processor

1. Combine ½ cup oil and 1 cup water in a saucepan, and bring to a boil. Remove pan from heat and add matzah meal, salt, and basil all at once. Stir well with wooden spoon.

2. Preheat oven to 375° F.

3. Insert metal blade. Place matzah meal mixture and eggs in work bowl and combine by pulsing 1 or 2 times. With machine running, drop 1 clove garlic through the feed tube. Process until mixture begins to form a ball.

4. Shape into an oval loaf. Place on ungreased cookie sheet and bake 40 to 50 minutes, until top is golden brown. Remove from cookie sheet and let cool 10 minutes on a rack. Split in half lengthwise.

5. Mince remaining clove of garlic and mix with 2 tablespoons oil; spread over each half. Toast under broiler. Cut into 12 slices and serve immediately.

Conventional

In step 3, chop garlic fine. Mix eggs and half of garlic into matzah-meal mixture by hand or with electric mixer.

Serves 6 to 12

Herb Bread (variation)

You will need 3 tablespoons of mixed herbs (such as oregano, rosemary, thyme, chives). Mix 2 tablespoons of the mixed herbs into the dough. In place of spreading garlic on the bread before toasting (in step 5), sprinkle with the remaining tablespoon of herbs.

Vegetable Muffins

2 small onions
2 stalks celery
1 cup fresh mushrooms
½ green pepper
3 tablespoons oil
1 clove garlic, cut in half
3 cups matzah farfel
2 cups chicken broth,
  heated
3 eggs, beaten
Salt and pepper to taste

Processor

1. Preheat oven to 350° F. Grease muffin tins.

2. Insert french fry blade; cut onions, celery, mushrooms, and green pepper to fit the feed tube. Using medium pressure, process onions and celery, then mushrooms and green pepper with light pressure.

3. Heat oil in a large skillet. Brown garlic clove, and remove. Add vegetables and brown quickly over high heat (2 to 3 minutes).

4. Soak farfel in warm chicken broth. Add vegetables and eggs. Season with salt and pepper, and mix well. Fill muffin tins.

5. Bake for 45 minutes or until golden brown. Let cool 5 minutes. Remove from pan and store in airtight container.

Conventional

In step 2, chop vegetables with a sharp knife.

Makes 15 to 20

Raisin Muffins

½ cup oil
1 cup sugar
3 eggs
½ cup matzah cake meal
¼ cup potato starch
Pinch of salt
½ cup raisins
½ cup sugar-cinnamon
  mixture

Processor

1. Preheat oven to 325° F. Place paper liners in muffin pan.

2. Insert metal blade. Put oil and sugar in work bowl and process for 5 seconds. Add eggs through feed tube, one at a time, with machine running.

3. Sift together cake meal, potato starch, and salt. Add to work bowl. Pulse 1 or 2 times until ingredients just disappear. Remove blade and fold in the raisins.

4. Fill muffin cups no more than three-fourths full. Sprinkle tops with cinnamon-sugar mixture. Bake for 40 to 50 minutes.

Conventional

In step 2, beat oil, sugar, and eggs with an electric mixer. In step 3, mix in dry ingredients by hand, and fold in the raisins.

Makes 12

Note: Apricots, prunes, currants, peaches, or any other type of dried fruit may be substituted for the raisins. Chop fruit, cover with hot water to soften, and drain well.

Banana Bread

5 eggs, separated
¾ cup sugar
¼ cup matzah cake meal
1 tablespoon potato
  starch
1 banana, cut into thirds
1 tablespoon orange juice
1 tablespoon grated
  orange peel
¼ cup white raisins

Processor

1. Preheat oven to 325° F. Grease two 7 7/8 x 3 7/8 loaf pans.

2. Insert metal blade. Place egg yolks and sugar in work bowl and process for 60 seconds until thick and pale yellow.

3. Sift together cake meal and potato starch. Add to work bowl along with banana, juice, and peel. Process until bananas just disappear. Remove to large bowl.

4. Soak raisins in hot water until softened. Drain and fold into batter.

5. Beat egg whites until stiff. Fold into batter.

6. Pour into pans. Bake for 1 hour. Let cool completely before removing from pans.

Conventional

In steps 2 and 3, beat egg yolks, sugar, banana, juice, and peel in electric mixer for 5 to 10 minutes. Add sifted dry ingredients. Proceed to step 4.

Makes 2 loaves

Soups

Cream of Broccoli Soup

1 small head broccoli
1 small green pepper
1 small onion
2 tablespoons butter or margarine
½ tablespoon potato starch
3 cups milk
1 cup half-and-half
¼ teaspoon nutmeg
1 teaspoon curry (optional)

Processor

1. Insert metal blade. Cut broccoli into 2-inch chunks and chop with 3 or 4 pulses. Set aside.

2. Change to french-fry blade. Cut green pepper and onion to fit feed tube. Process.

3. Heat butter in a 2-quart saucepan, and saute pepper and onion until soft, about 5 minutes.

4. Combine potato starch, milk, and half-and-half. Add to saucepan along with broccoli, nutmeg, and curry. Bring to a boil, lower heat, and simmer for 20 minutes, stirring occasionally. Serve hot or cold.

Conventional

Chop vegetables by hand and proceed to step 3.

Serves 4 to 6

Cabbage Borscht

1 pound short ribs
1 pound soup meat
1 knucklebone
3 marrow bones
1 large head of cabbage
4 small yellow onions
15-ounce can tomatoes
½ cup ketchup (or to
    taste)
½ cup white sugar
½ cup brown sugar
Juice of 2 lemons
Salt and pepper to taste

This soup must be made at least one day ahead. Served with some wonderful Passover garlic bread, it's a meal in itself.

Processor

1. Wash meat and bones and place in an 8-quart pot with 4 quarts of water.

2. Insert grater blade. Cut cabbage into quarters and remove the thick core; grate, and place in soup pot.

3. Change to metal blade. Place onions, tomatoes, ketchup, sugars, and lemon juice in work bowl, and chop. Add to pot.

4. Cover pot and bring to boil. Lower to simmer and cook 3 to 4 hours. Remove from heat and let cool. Refrigerate overnight.

5. The next day, skim off the congealed fat. Remove marrow and meat from bones; cut meat into small pieces and return to pot. Season with salt and pepper, and reheat over low heat for 30 minutes.

Conventional

In steps 2 and 3, grate vegetables by hand.

Serves 10 to 12

Cream of Cauliflower Soup Plus

1 small head cauliflower
2 carrots, peeled
1 parsnip, peeled
1 turnip, peeled
1 zucchini
1 leek (white part only)
2 stalks celery
4 cups milk
½ teaspoon ground
  nutmeg
Several drops of almond
  flavoring
2 tablespoons potato
  starch
1 small onion, cut in half
3 tablespoons butter or
  margarine
Juice of 1 lemon
Salt and white pepper to
  taste
Chopped chives for
  garnish

Processor

1. Break cauliflower into small flowerets. Cut carrots, parsnip, turnip, zucchini, and leek into 4 pieces each. String the celery with a vegetable peeler; cut into 2-inch pieces and set aside.

2. Place cauliflower, carrots, parsnip, turnip, zucchini, and leek in ½ cup boiling water in a large pot; cover, and cook for 10 to 15 minutes. Strain off liquid and add enough water to make 1 cup; set aside.

3. Insert metal blade. Process the cooked vegetables in batches until smooth and well blended, stopping occasionally to scrape down sides. Remove to a bowl.

4. Pour milk into a pitcher; add nutmeg and almond flavoring. Stir in potato starch.

5. With processor running, drop onion and celery through feed tube and mince well.

6. Heat butter in a large soup pot. Saute onion and celery with lemon juice for 2 minutes. Season with salt and pepper. Add milk and reserved vegetable liquid. Let come to a slow boil, stir in processed vegetables, and continue stirring. Turn to simmer and let thicken with lid off.

7. When ready to serve, check seasonings and thickness of soup. Depending on how rich or how thick you want it, you may need to add more milk. Sprinkle with chopped chives and serve hot.

Conventional

Follow processor instructions, chopping vegetables by hand, and pureeing soup in a blender.

Serves 4 to 6

Blender Beet Borscht

32-ounce jar borscht with
  beets
1 medium cucumber,
  peeled and seeded
2 small green onions
1 cup sour cream
Salt and pepper to taste
Sour cream for topping

This recipe does not work well in a food processor because it may spill over.

1. Pour half of the borscht from the jar into the blender. Cut cucumber and onions into 2-inch pieces and add with half of the sour cream. Blend on low speed for 10 seconds and high speed for 5 seconds. Pour into a large bowl.

2. Pour remaining borscht from the jar and remaining sour cream into the blender and blend on low speed for 10 seconds and high speed for 5 seconds. Add to bowl. Season with salt and pepper.

3. Serve cold in mugs with a dollop of sour cream, or serve warm and pass the sour cream.

Serves 8

Mushroom Soup Supreme

½ pound fresh
  mushrooms, sliced
½ stick (¼ cup) unsalted
  butter
¼ cup sherry
4-ounce box mushroom
  soup mix
½ pint whipping cream
  or half-and-half

1. Heat butter in a medium skillet and saute mushrooms. Add sherry and cook for 2 or 3 minutes. Set aside.

2. Prepare soup mix according to directions on package, using only 3 cups of water. When soup comes to boil, add mushrooms, turn to simmer, and stir in cream. Serve immediately.

Serves 6 to 8

Garlic Soup

1 large head of garlic,
  unpeeled
6 cups beef stock (you
  may use any leftover
  beef gravy as part of
  this)
1 small onion, chopped
¼ cup chopped fresh
  parsley
1 tablespoon ketchup
¼ teaspoon thyme
1 bay leaf
Salt and pepper to taste
1 egg

1. Separate garlic head into cloves. Place in a 4-quart soup pot, add 4 cups boiling water, and boil 30 minutes. Drain off water, run garlic under cold water, and remove peel.

2. Return garlic to soup pot. Add beef stock, onion, parsley, ketchup, thyme, and bay leaf. Season with salt and pepper. Bring to a boil, turn to simmer, and cook for 20 minutes. Before serving, return to boil and beat in egg.

Serves 8 to 10

Cold Cucumber Soup

4 large cucumbers,
  peeled and seeded
1 cup fresh parsley
2 green onions
2 tablespoons unsalted
  butter or margarine
1 tablespoon salt
1 tablespoon white
  pepper
1½ quarts sour milk
1 pint heavy cream
Chopped mint or sliced
  radishes for garnish

Processor

1. Select firm cucumbers. Cut into 1-inch pieces. Trim stems from parsley. Cut onion into 1-inch pieces.

2. Insert metal blade. Place cucumbers, parsley, and onions in work bowl and chop finely with several pulses.

3. Heat butter in a skillet, and saute vegetables for 1 or 2 minutes. Season with salt and pepper. Cover pan and cook 3 to 5 minutes or until cucumber is soft. Drain.

4. Combine milk, cream, and vegetables. Process in batches until smooth. Chill for several hours or overnight.

5. Adjust seasoning. Serve cold with chopped mint or sliced radishes.

Conventional

Follow processor instructions, chopping vegetables by hand, and pureeing soup in a blender.

Makes 2 quarts; serves 8 to 10

Smartini Soup

1 small cucumber, peeled
and seeded
3 stalks celery, cut into
2-inch pieces
1 cup milk
½ cup sour cream
1 teaspoon chives
8 ice cubes
1 teaspoon fresh chopped
mint for garnish

This soup is cool and delicious.

Processor

1. Insert metal blade. Cut cucumber into chunks and place in work bowl; pulse 4 or 5 times to chop. Reserve.

2. Place celery in work bowl, and chop until fine. Add milk, sour cream, and chives, and process for 10 seconds. Add ice cubes and process for 30 seconds. Scrape down sides of bowl and process 30 seconds more.

3. Pour into serving bowl, stir in cucumber, and garnish with chopped mint. Serve immediately.

Conventional

Cut up cucumber and celery by hand. You can use a blender to chop the ice cubes and vegetables, and mix the soup, but it will have a different consistency.

Serves 4 to 6

Gazpacho

1 small onion
1 medium cucumber,
 peeled and seeded
½ cup fresh chives
1 medium green pepper
3 stalks celery, strings
 removed
3 ripe tomatoes, peeled
 and seeded
½ cup fresh chives
1 large clove garlic
3 cups tomato juice
2 tablespoons oil
1 tablespoon lemon juice
1 teaspoon salt
¼ teaspoon ground black
 pepper

Processor

1. Insert metal blade. Cut up onion, cucumber, and chives and place in work bowl; chop with 3 pulses. Cut green pepper and celery into 2-inch chunks and add to work bowl. Pulse 3 times. Set aside.

2. Cut tomatoes into quarters, and chop with 3 pulses. Add to chopped vegetables.

3. Drop garlic clove through feed tube with processor running. Return 2 cups of the chopped vegetables to the work bowl.

4. Combine tomato juice, oil, lemon juice, salt, and pepper; add through the feed tube with processor running. Process 5 seconds to blend well. Pour over remaining (unprocessed) chopped vegetables. Refrigerate for several hours before serving.

Conventional

Chop vegetables with a sharp knife or food mill. Mince the garlic and continue with step 4, blending vegetables and liquid with a blender.

Serves 6 to 8

Egg Drop Soup

See Seder Menu #1 for recipe.

Chicken Soup with Matzah Balls

4- to 5-pound stewing
  chicken (with giblets),
  cut into 8 pieces
1 large onion
3 cloves
1 large parsnip, peeled
¼ stalk celery with leaves
Several sprigs of fresh
  parsley
1 teaspoon salt
¼ teaspoon pepper
Matzah Balls (recipe
  follows)

Some traditional dishes still use traditional methods. This is one of them.

1. Clean the chicken pieces in cold water. Make sure all the pinheads are removed. Place in a 6-quart soup pot.

2. Stick the onion with cloves. Place in pot with the parsnip, celery, parsley, salt, and pepper. Add water to cover and bring to a boil.

3. Skim the top of the soup and cover pot. Turn heat to simmer and cook slowly for 2 to 3 hours.

4. Cool. Discard the onion, celery, and parsley. Remove chicken (save for another use). Refrigerate broth overnight. To serve, remove congealed fat, add matzah balls, and reheat for at least 15 minutes.

Serves 12 to 14

Matzah Balls

3 large eggs, separated
½ teaspoon salt
Dash of white pepper
¼ teaspoon cinnamon
¾ cup matzah meal

Some matzah balls sink to the bottom of the bowl and are hard to cut. Others are light, melt in your mouth, and float. This foolproof recipe, which belonged to my husband's Great Aunt Lizzie, will always give you "floaters"! What makes the matzah balls float is whipping air into the egg whites and then folding them gently into the yolks so the mixture does not break down.

1. Combine the egg yolks with salt, pepper, and cinnamon in a medium bowl.
2. In another bowl, beat the egg whites until stiff but not dry. Fold them slowly into the egg yolk mixture with a rubber spatula.
3. Slowly fold in the matzah meal, ¼ cup at a time; it should be absorbed but still hold air and not become thick like paste. You may not need the entire ¾ cup; it all depends on the size of the yolks. Cover and refrigerate.
4. Bring a 4-quart pot of water to a boil, then remove the matzah-ball mixture from the refrigerator. Moisten your hands with cold water and form balls, dropping them into the boiling water. Cover the pot, turn the heat to simmer, and cook for about 40 minutes.
5. Remove the matzah balls with a slotted spoon. When cool, add them to the chicken soup. Simmer for 15 minutes before serving.

Makes 12 large or about 18 small matzah balls.

Note: Matzah balls can be made several days ahead. For color, add ¼ teaspoon chopped parsley to the egg yolk mixture. They may be used in any type of broth, or served hot as a substitute for potatoes.

Apricot-Yogurt Soup

17-ounce can apricot halves
2 cups orange juice or apricot nectar
1 cup apricot preserves
¼ cup fresh lime juice
16-ounce carton plain yogurt
Toasted almonds for garnish

Making a variety of soups from fruits is one way to give your palate a new experience. This one is nice served in mugs as an appetizer.

Processor

1. Insert metal blade. Empty apricots and syrup from can into work bowl and process for 3 seconds. Add orange juice, apricot preserves, lime juice, and 1 cup water and process until smooth, about 10 seconds. Pour into a large bowl. (You may have to do this in batches.)

2. Fold in yogurt. Chill at least 3 hours. Garnish with toasted almonds.

Conventional

You can use a blender to chop the apricots and mix the soup, but it will have a different consistency and flavor.

Serves 6 to 8

Cream of Cantaloupe Soup

2 cups cantaloupe, cut
   into 1-inch cubes
1 cup orange juice
Juice and grated peel of 1
   lemon
½ teaspoon cinnamon
½ cup heavy cream
2 tablespoons honey
Dash of cumin
16-ounce carton peach
   yogurt
¼ cup chopped mint for
   garnish

Processor

1. Insert metal blade. Place cantaloupe in work bowl; process for 10 seconds. Add orange juice, lemon juice, lemon peel, and cinnamon. Process 10 seconds.

2. Add cream, honey, and cumin and process until smooth, scraping down sides of bowl as necessary. Remove from bowl and fold in yogurt.

3. Refrigerate for several hours. To serve, sprinkle with chopped mint.

Conventional

You can use a blender to chop the cantaloupe and mix the soup, but it will have a different consistency.

Serves 6 to 8

Avocado-Banana Soup

2 ripe avocados, cut into
   chunks
2 large bananas, cut into
   chunks
1 cup milk
1 cup sugar
4 tablespoons lemon juice
1 teaspoon cinnamon
32 ounces plain yogurt
Grated nutmeg for
   garnish

Processor

1. Insert metal blade. Process avocados and bananas for 10 seconds. Add milk, sugar, lemon juice, and cinnamon, and process for 15 seconds. Scrape down sides of bowl and process 15 seconds more. Pour into a bowl.

2. Mix in yogurt. Chill 3 hours. To serve, sprinkle with grated nutmeg.

Conventional

The ingredients may be mashed and combined in a blender or by hand. Proceed to step 2.

Serves 6 to 8

Strawberry Soup

1 quart fresh
strawberries, stems
removed
¾ cup dry red wine
½ cup sugar
2 tablespoons lemon juice
1 teaspoon cinnamon
½ cup whipping cream
¼ cup sour cream

Microwave

1. Puree the strawberries in food processor or with a food mill. Set aside.

2. Combine wine, sugar, lemon juice, and cinnamon with 1 ½ cups water in a 6-cup microwave-safe container. Microwave on high for 8 minutes. Stir after 5 minutes. Add strawberry puree and microwave for 5 minutes. Cool.

3. Whip cream until stiff. Combine with sour cream and fold into the strawberry puree. Serve at room temperature.

Conventional

In step 2, combine wine, sugar, lemon juice, and cinnamon with 1 ½ cups water in a medium saucepan and cook for 15 minutes, uncovered, stirring occasionally. Add the strawberry puree and cook 10 minutes, stirring frequently. Proceed to step 3.

Serves 8 to 10

Salads

Three Pepper Salad

4 medium sweet peppers
  (red, yellow, and green
  if possible)
1 clove garlic, chopped
½ cup oil
3 tablespoons lemon juice
Salt and pepper to taste
1 green onion
Green olives for garnish

1. Preheat broiler. Broil whole peppers about 6 inches from the heat source, turning often, until skins are uniformly charred. Place peppers in a plastic bag. Seal tightly and let steam for 10 minutes.

2. Remove peppers from bag and discard skins, stem ends, and seeds. Cut into 1- or 2-inch strips about ¼ inch wide. Place in refrigerator until 30 minutes before serving. (Steps 1 and 2 may be done a day or two in advance.)

3. Combine garlic, oil, lemon juice, salt, and pepper. Pour over prepared peppers and marinate at room temperature until serving time.

4. Cut the green onion into thin diagonal slices and sprinkle over the peppers. Garnish with olives.

Serves 6

Red and White Cole Slaw

2-pound head of red
  cabbage
2-pound head of green
  cabbage
1 large green pepper
8 stalks celery with leaves
4 carrots, peeled
10 green onions
1½ cups mayonnaise
1 teaspoon sugar
4 tablespoons vinegar
1 tablespoon fresh
  tarragon
Salt and pepper to taste

Processor (make in batches if you have a small processor)

1. Insert medium slicing blade. Core cabbage, and cut to fit the feed tube. Slice, using firm pressure. Set aside. Cut green pepper, celery, and carrots to fit the feed tube. Slice.

2. Change to metal blade. Cut green onions into 2-inch pieces and add to work bowl. Chop with 2 or 3 pulses, scraping bowl as needed. Remove vegetables to a large bowl.

3. Place 2 to 3 cups of cabbage at a time in the work bowl and chop with 3 or 4 pulses. Continue until all the cabbage has been chopped. Add to chopped vegetables.

4. Process mayonnaise, sugar, vinegar, and tarragon 4 to 6 seconds, until well mixed. Pour over slaw and mix well. Season with salt and pepper. Refrigerate until ready to serve.

Conventional

Shred cabbage with a sharp knife. Chop green pepper, celery, carrots, and green onions. Combine the dressing ingredients and mix into cabbage.

Serves 12 to 16

Israeli Salad

1 carrot
3 radishes
1 small red onion
1 small green pepper
1 cucumber, peeled and
  seeded
2 green onions
1 tablespoon parsley
3 medium tomatoes,
  seeded
1 tablespoon oil
1 tablespoon lemon juice
Pinch of salt
Pepper to taste

Processor

1. Insert grater blade, and cut carrot to fit feed tube. Grate carrot and radishes. Set aside.

2. Change to french-fry blade. Cut onion, green pepper, and cucumber to fit the feed tube. Process, and add to carrots.

3. Change to metal blade. Cut green onions into 2-inch pieces. Process green onions and parsley until chopped well, about 2 or 3 pulses. Add to vegetables. Cut tomatoes in half and chop with 3 or 4 pulses. Scrape bowl as necessary. Add to vegetables. Refrigerate for several hours.

4. Thirty minutes before serving, make dressing by mixing together the oil, lemon juice, salt, and pepper. Pour over vegetables and let marinate until ready to serve.

Conventional

Chop vegetables with a sharp knife (do not mince). Chop green onion and parsley quite fine. Proceed to step 4.

Serves 4

Avocado and Grapefruit Salad with Honey Dressing

See Seder Menu #1 for recipe.

Cucumber Salad

4 medium cucumbers,
  peeled, seeded, and
  sliced
1 teaspoon salt
¼ cup vinegar
1 tablespoon white wine
1 teaspoon sugar
¼ teaspoon black pepper
1 medium onion, sliced
½ cup sour cream

This salad is very easy to make. The thinner the cucumber and the fewer the seeds, the better the taste. My dad taught me a special trick that gives it a top-notch flavor.

1. Sprinkle cucumbers with salt, and refrigerate for 2 hours. Cover the top with a plate to weigh down the cucumber. (This is my dad's special trick, which removes the excess water and the bitterness.) Drain.

2. Combine vinegar, wine, sugar, and pepper. Add with the onion. Refrigerate for at least 1 hour. When ready to serve, fold in the sour cream and enjoy!

Serves 8

Bibb Lettuce Salad with Vinaigrette

2 heads bibb lettuce
½ cup oil
2 tablespoons vinegar
2 tablespoons dry red
  wine
1 tablespoon chopped
  chives
1 teaspoon salt
¼ teaspoon freshly
  ground pepper

1. Wash lettuce under cold water. Towel dry, place in salad bowl, and wrap with paper towels. Refrigerate.

2. Combine the remaining ingredients for the dressing.

3. Serve lettuce with 1 or 2 tablespoons dressing per serving.

Serves 6 to 8; makes about ¾ cup dressing

Salad Hints

1. Wash, dry (use a salad spinner if possible), and store your greens in the refrigerator in a plastic bag or in a large bowl with some paper towels on the bottom. Cover, and place greens in the crisper of your refrigerator.

2. Use the metal blade of your processor for dressings and chopped vegetables, using quick on/off pulses. Use the slicer blade for celery, onions, mushrooms, and peppers.

3. Keep a bowl of raw, cut-up vegetables (but not tomatoes) in your refrigerator for last-minute salad making.

4. To keep lettuce from wilting, don't add dressing to your salad until you're ready to serve.

5. What to put in a tossed green salad: When we think of tossed green salad we mainly think of lettuce, with several vegetables as garnishes or accents. With so many varieties of greens in the markets today, it's nice to serve several in a salad. Mix any of the following for a lovely tossed green salad that's different. Serve with the dressing of your choice.

Greens

Bibb lettuce	Head lettuce (iceberg)
Boston lettuce	Leaf lettuce (red or green)
Celery cabbage	Spinach leaves
Endive	Watercress
Escarole	

Accompaniments

Bell peppers (green or red)	Onions (red or white)
Celery	Radishes
Cherry tomatoes	Raw vegetables (broccoli, carrots,
Cucumbers	cauliflower florets, zucchini)
Mushrooms (fresh or	Scallions (green onions)
marinated)	Tomatoes
Olives	

Farmer's Chop Suey

2 green onions, cut in 2-inch pieces
32 ounces creamed cottage cheese
16 ounces sour cream
1 cucumber, peeled and seeded
1 green pepper
6 small radishes
2 ripe tomatoes, cut into 8 pieces
1 teaspoon salt
¼ teaspoon white pepper

This recipe is subtitled "Garden Vegetables and Cottage Cheese."

Processor

1. Insert metal blade. Chop onions. Add cottage cheese and sour cream to work bowl and process for 5 seconds, until well blended, scraping down the sides of bowl when necessary. Remove to a large serving bowl.
2. Change to french-fry blade. Cut the cucumber and green pepper to fit the feed tube and cut with medium pressure. Add the radishes to feed tube and cut with firm pressure. Add to cottage cheese mixture.
3. Add tomatoes, salt, and pepper. Mix well. Refrigerate for several hours before serving.

Conventional

Chop green onion; add to cottage cheese and sour cream. Mix well. Cube remaining vegetables except tomatoes and proceed to step 3.

Serves 6

Chicken Salad

1 ½ cups cooked chicken breast, cubed
1 ½ cups fresh mushrooms (about ½ lb.), sliced
1 teaspoon finely chopped onion
1 cup chopped celery (about 3 stalks)
6 to 8 green olives, chopped
⅓ cup mayonnaise
1 tablespoon lemon juice
½ teaspoon salt

Combine chicken, mushrooms, onion, celery, and olives in a large bowl. Combine mayonnaise, lemon juice, and salt, and add to chicken mixture. Mix lightly with a fork. Chill thoroughly. Serve on lettuce.

Serves 6

Hot Potato Salad Lyonnaise Style

3 tablespoons oil
2 tablespoons chicken broth
2 tablespoons dry white wine
1 tablespoon lemon juice
1 tablespoon vinegar
1/4 teaspoon salt
Freshly ground black pepper
6 Idaho potatoes, peeled and sliced
2 tablespoons chopped green onions
1 tablespoon chopped fresh parsley

Microwave

Combine oil, chicken broth, wine, lemon juice, vinegar, salt, and pepper in a 2-quart microwave-safe casserole. Microwave on high setting for 1 minute. Stir well. Add potatoes and cover with vented plastic wrap. Cook on high setting for 6 minutes. Stir, cover again, and cook for 5 or 6 minutes on high until potatoes are tender. Let stand, covered, for 10 minutes. Sprinkle with green onions and parsley.

Conventional

Cook the potatoes in a 1-quart saucepan with 1/2 cup boiling water 15 to 20 minutes or until tender. Drain. Place in serving bowl with chopped green onions and parsley. Bring remaining ingredients to boil in a small saucepan. Pour over potatoes and sprinkle with green onions and parsley.

Serves 8 to 10

Hot Tuna Salad

12-ounce can tuna (water pack)
4 hard-cooked eggs, chopped
2 stalks celery, chopped
1 small onion, chopped
8 to 10 green olives, chopped
1 cup matzah farfel
1 cup sour cream
¾ cup mayonnaise
½ teaspoon horseradish
½ teaspoon salt
Dash of pepper
¼ teaspoon curry
½ cup grated sharp cheese

1. Rinse tuna with cold water. Flake with a fork. Add eggs, celery, onion, and olives.

2. Soak farfel in ½ cup warm water until most of the water is absorbed. Squeeze out excess and combine with tuna mixture.

3. Combine sour cream, mayonnaise, horseradish, salt, pepper, and curry. Add to tuna mixture.

4. Spoon into 8 individual scallop shell baking dishes (or a 2-quart casserole). Sprinkle with grated cheese and refrigerate for 1 hour or until ready to bake.

5. Place shells in a circle in microwave, 1-inch apart; cover with plastic wrap or wax paper and microwave on reheat setting for 12 minutes. Or bake in a 350° oven for 30 minutes.

Serves 8

Molded Spinach Salad

1 pound fresh spinach
(or 10-ounce box frozen
spinach)
2 stalks celery, cut into
1-inch pieces
2 green onions, cut into
1-inch pieces
½ cup mayonnaise
2 boxes (3 oz. each)
kosher lemon gelatin*
1 ½ tablespoons vinegar
¾ cup small-curd cottage
cheese
Sour Cream Dressing
(recipe follows)

Processor

1. Wash spinach thoroughly and drain. Place in large pot (do not add liquid). Cover, and cook until wilted, about 5 to 8 minutes. Squeeze dry.
2. Grease a 1-quart mold or loaf pan.
3. Insert metal blade. Place celery and green onions in work bowl and chop with 2 pulses. Add spinach and chop with 2 or 3 pulses. Remove to a large bowl.
4. Place mayonnaise, gelatin, and vinegar in work bowl with 1 ½ cups boiling water. Process for 5 seconds. Add to vegetables and mix together. Fold in cottage cheese. Pour into mold and chill in refrigerator until firm.
5. When ready to serve, run a knife around inside of pan and invert. Serve on lettuce leaves with Sour Cream Dressing.

Conventional

In step 3, chop vegetables with a sharp knife. In step 4, combine hot water, mayonnaise, gelatin, and vinegar; stir until gelatin dissolves.

Serves 6 to 8

*Kosher gelatin gels differently from non-kosher gelatin. See conversion table.

Sour Cream Dressing

1 cup sour cream or
yogurt
1 tablespoon lemon juice
1 tablespoon honey or
sugar
¼ cup cream

Blend all ingredients in food processor (using plastic blade) or beat with wire whisk. Refrigerate. Makes about 1½ cups.

Avocado Mousse

2 tablespoons kosher
  unflavored gelatin*
3-ounce box kosher lime
  gelatin*
2 medium avocados
½-inch piece lemon peel
½ cup mayonnaise
½ cup sour cream
½ cup heavy cream

Processor

1. Insert metal blade. Place both gelatins in work bowl with 1 cup plus 2 tablespoons boiling water. Process for 5 seconds. Place in refrigerator to thicken.

2. Peel avocados and cut in half. Add to work bowl and process for 30 seconds, stopping to scrape bowl as necessary. Add lemon peel and mayonnaise and process 15 seconds. Stir into thickened gelatin.

3. Fold in sour cream and heavy cream. Pour into a mold greased with mayonnaise and refrigerate until set. Unmold, and serve on salad greens.

Conventional

In step 1, stir gelatin in boiling water until dissolved. In step 2, mash avocado with a fork or potato masher; grate the lemon peel. Proceed to step 3.

Serves 8

Molded Pineapple-Cucumber Salad

2 packages (3 oz. each)
  kosher lime gelatin*
2 ½ cups crushed
  pineapple
1 small cucumber,
  peeled, seeded, and
  chopped
1 cup sour cream
Cherry tomatoes (for
  center of ring mold)

1. Dissolve gelatin in 2 ½ cups of boiling water. Add pineapple and cucumber. Mix in 1 cup of cold water. Chill until thickened (about 1 hour).

2. Mix in sour cream, and spoon into a greased 1 ½-quart ring mold. Chill until set. Fill the center with cherry tomatoes.

Serves 10 to 12

*Kosher gelatin gels differently from non-kosher gelatin. See conversion table.

Tomato-Vegetable Aspic

3-ounce package kosher
  lemon gelatin*
2 tablespoons kosher
  unflavored gelatin*
¼ cup vinegar
14-ounce can tomatoes
½ teaspoon horseradish
Salt and pepper to taste
1 small cucumber, peeled
  and seeded
2 stalks celery
½ green pepper

Processor

1. Bring 1¼ cups water to boil; add lemon gelatin, unflavored gelatin, and vinegar, and cook and stir over medium heat for 5 minutes.

2. Insert metal blade. Place tomatoes, horseradish, salt, and pepper in the work'bowl and process for 5 seconds. Add to hot gelatin mixture, stirring well. Cook for 5 minutes. Remove from heat and chill until thickened.

3. Change to french-fry blade. Cut cucumber, celery, and green pepper to fit the feed tube. Process, then fold into gelatin mixture.

4. Grease a 1½-quart ring mold with oil, and spoon in vegetable mixture. Refrigerate until firm, about 2 hours. Unmold to serve.

Conventional

In step 2, combine the ingredients with an electric mixer. In step 3, chop the vegetables with a sharp knife. Proceed to step 4.

Serves 6 to 8

*Kosher gelatin gels differently from non-kosher gelatin. See conversion table.

Papaya Bowl

2 bananas, sliced
1 papaya, peeled, seeded, cubed
½ fresh pineapple, cubed
¼ cup chopped walnuts or macadamia nuts
1 small head lettuce, shredded
Coconut Dressing (recipe follows)

1. Toss fruits and nuts together.

2. Arrange lettuce in serving dish and place fruit and nut mixture on top.

3. Add dressing just before serving.

Serves 4

Coconut Dressing

¼ cup honey
2 tablespoons lemon juice
⅔ cup mayonnaise
¼ teaspoon ground ginger
⅓ cup grated coconut (toasted optional)

Blend all ingredients in food processor or shake in a jar. Makes 1 cup.

Vegetables

Spinach Souffle

2 tablespoons soup nut
  crumbs (divided)
2 packages (10 oz. each)
  frozen spinach
1½ tablespoons butter or
  margarine
¾ tablespoon potato
  starch
1 egg, separated
2 eggs, whole
½ cup mayonnaise
1 teaspoon ground
  nutmeg
½ teaspoon salt
Dash of pepper

Processor

1. Preheat oven to 350° F. Grease a 4-cup souffle dish or 7 x 11½ baking dish and dust with 1 tablespoon crumbs.

2. Cook spinach according to package directions. Drain reserving ¾ cup of the liquid.

3. Insert metal blade. Chop spinach 10 to 15 seconds.

4. Melt butter in a 1-quart saucepan. Add potato starch and make a roux by slowly adding reserved spinach liquid and stirring constantly with a wire whisk until smooth. Remove from heat and beat in 1 egg yolk.

5. Combine remaining eggs and egg white, mayonnaise, nutmeg, salt, and pepper in work bowl. With machine running, add potato starch mixture through feed tube and process just until blended. Add to chopped spinach. Mix well. Pour into souffle dish and dust with remaining crumbs.

6. Bake for 40 to 50 minutes until puffed and golden. Serve at once .

Serves 4 to 6.

Creamed Spinach

10-ounce package frozen
  spinach
1 tablespoon potato
  starch
2 tablespoons butter or
  margarine
½ teaspoon salt
¼ teaspoon nutmeg

Processor

1. Cook spinach according to package directions. Drain well and reserve liquid. Add
   water to liquid to make ¾ cup. Set aside.
2. Insert metal blade. Chop spinach for 15
   to 20 seconds.
3. Dissolve potato starch in 2 tablespoons
   cold water. Heat butter in small saucepan,
   add potato starch, and whisk until well
   blended. Add salt, nutmeg, and ¾ cup
   spinach liquid. Cook, stirring constantly,
   until sauce becomes smooth and begins to
   thicken. Add spinach and stir well. Serve
   hot.

Conventional

Follow processor instructions, chopping spinach by hand.

Serves 4

Spinach-Vegetable Squares

3 large carrots
10-ounce package frozen
spinach, thawed
1 medium onion, cut in
quarters
2 medium green peppers,
cut in quarters
2 stalks celery, cut into
2-inch pieces
1 cup bouillon (beef,
vegetable, or chicken)
3 eggs
¾ cup matzah meal
Salt and pepper to taste

Processor

1. Preheat oven to 350° F. Grease an 8-inch square pan.

2. Insert grater blade. Grate carrots and set aside.

3. Change to metal blade. Chop spinach, onion, green pepper, and celery with 2 pulses. Place in a 2-quart saucepan. Add grated carrots and bouillon. Cook over medium heat for 15 to 20 minutes until vegetables are soft and liquid is reduced to ¼ cup.

4. Place eggs and matzah meal in work bowl and process for 30 seconds. Stir into cooked vegetables. Season with salt and pepper. Spread mixture evenly in baking pan. Bake, uncovered, for 45 minutes. Cut into squares.

Conventional

Follow processor instructions, chopping and grating vegetables by hand. In step 4, beat together eggs and matzah meal with rotary or electric mixer until eggs are frothy.

Serves 9

Greek Vegetable Casserole

1 eggplant (1 lb.)
Salt
16-ounce can tomatoes,
  drained
1½ pounds potatoes,
  peeled
1½ pounds zucchini
½ cup fresh parsley
½ cup fresh dill (or 3
  Tbsp. dried)
Salt and freshly ground
  pepper to taste
5 green onions, cut into
  2-inch pieces
3 cloves garlic
2 fresh tomatoes, cut in
  quarters
2 tablespoons oil
2 packages (10 oz. each)
  frozen okra, thawed
¼ cup soup nut crumbs

Processor

1. Slice the eggplant, salt each slice thoroughly on both sides, and set aside. Cut canned tomatoes into small pieces with a sharp knife.

2. Insert medium slicing blade. Cut potatoes and zucchini to fit feed tube and slice with firm pressure. Set aside.

3. Change to metal blade, Chop parsley and dill with 3 or 4 pulses. Add to potato mixture with canned tomatoes. Season with salt and pepper. Mix thoroughly.

4. With the machine running, drop the green onions and garlic cloves through the feed tube. Add the fresh tomatoes and process for 3 seconds.

5. Heat the oil in a small pan. Saute the fresh tomato mixture, then simmer uncovered for 10 minutes.

6. Preheat the oven to 350°F. Rinse the eggplant slices in cold water. Pat dry with paper towels.

7. In a 4-quart ungreased casserole, layer the vegetables as follows: potato mixture, okra, and eggplant. Spoon the sauteed vegetables over the top and sprinkle with the soup nut crumbs. Bake for 1 hour.

Conventional

Follow processor instructions, slicing and chopping vegetables with a sharp knife.

Serves 6 to 8

Julienne Vegetables

4 medium zucchini
2 stalks celery
5 medium carrots
1 ½ teaspoons salt
(divided)
6 tablespoons butter or
margarine
1 tablespoon lemon juice
¼ teaspoon nutmeg
Pinch of sugar
Pinch of white pepper

Conventional

1. Cut zucchini, celery, and carrots into very thin julienne strips (preferably using a food processor with the french fry blade).

2. Bring 2 quarts of water to a boil; add 1 teaspoon salt. Place zucchini and celery in a strainer and immerse in the boiling water for 2 minutes. Remove and rinse under cold running water. Repeat with carrots for 3 minutes. (The vegetables may be cooked ahead in the morning and held until dinner time.)

3. Combine ½ teaspoon salt, lemon juice, nutmeg, sugar, and pepper. Melt butter in a skillet on medium heat, and stir in vegetables and seasonings. Cook until heated through.

Microwave

In step 1, place all vegetables in a 4-quart microwave-safe baking dish with ½ cup water and cook on high setting for 5 minutes. Remove, drain, and rinse under cold running water to stop the cooking.

Serves 4 to 6

Eggplant Fritters

See Seder Menu #2 for recipe.

Zucchini

1 small green pepper
3 zucchini
2 cloves garlic
1 shallot
2 tablespoons oil
1 teaspoon fresh basil (or
   ⅓ tsp. dried)
1 teaspoon fresh oregano
   (or ⅓ tsp. dried)
Salt and pepper to taste
½ cup white wine

Processor

1. Insert slicing blade. Slice green pepper and set aside. Slice zucchini and set aside.

2. Change to metal blade. With processor running, drop garlic and shallot through the feed tube. Add to green pepper.

3. Heat oil in medium skillet. Saute green pepper, garlic, and shallot about 3 minutes. Remove to small bowl. Add zucchini to skillet with basil and oregano; saute 3 minutes. Cover and cook 5 minutes. Add to green peppers and mix well. Season with salt and pepper. Remove to serving dish.

4. Add wine to skillet over high heat, and reduce liquid to ¼ cup, scraping skillet. Pour over zucchini and serve at once.

Conventional

Follow processor instructions, slicing and chopping Vegetables with a sharp knife.

Serves 2

Baked Tomato Slices with Puffed Cheese Topping

2 firm ripe tomatoes,
   about 3" diameter
Salt and pepper to taste
½ cup soup nut crumbs
3 tablespoons oil
1 tablespoon chopped
   fresh basil
½ cup mayonnaise
1 egg white
3 tablespoons grated
   parmesan cheese
2 teaspoons horseradish

1. Preheat oven to 425° F.

2. Slice tomatoes into 1-inch slices; you should have 2 slices from each tomato. Place in a baking dish. Season with salt and pepper.

3. Combine crumbs, oil, and basil. Spread on the tomato slices. Combine mayonnaise, egg white, grated cheese, and horseradish; drop a large tablespoon of mixture on each tomato slice.

4. Bake until topping is puffed and brown, about 10 to 15 minutes. Serve immediately.

Serves 4

Baked Tomatoes with Basil

2 firm, ripe tomatoes
(about 3″ diameter)
Salt and pepper to taste
½ cup soup nut crumbs
3 tablespoons oil
1 clove garlic, minced
4 thin slices red onion
1 tablespoon chopped
fresh basil (or 1 tsp.
dried)

1. Preheat oven to 350° F.
2. Slice tomatoes into 1-inch slices. You should get 2 slices from each tomato. Place in a baking dish. Season with salt and pepper.
3. Combine crumbs, oil, and garlic. Spread mixture on tomato slices. Top with a slice of onion. Sprinkle evenly with basil.
4. Bake, uncovered, for 15 minutes. Or microwave, covered loosely, on high setting for 2 to 3 minutes, until heated through; let stand, covered, for 1 minute.

Serves 2 to 4.

Stewed Tomato Pudding

3½ cups canned
tomatoes
1½ cups matzah farfel
⅓ cup melted butter or
margarine
1 cup sugar
1 teaspoon cinnamon
1 teaspoon ground ginger
½ teaspoon salt
Dash of pepper

This is a great side dish!

Processor

1. Preheat oven to 350° F. Grease a 1 ½-quart baking dish. Drain tomatoes, reserving liquid.
2. Place farfel and melted butter in the baking dish and toss lightly with a fork.
3. Insert metal blade. Place tomatoes in work bowl with sugar, cinnamon, ginger, salt, and pepper. Process until smooth, about 10 seconds, stopping to scrape down sides of bowl. Transfer to a saucepan, add tomato liquid, and bring to a boil. Remove from heat and pour over farfel. Bake uncovered for about 45 minutes.

Conventional

Follow processor instructions, chopping tomatoes with a knife.

Serves 6

Brussels Sprouts Timbales

18 ounces brussels
sprouts
2 tablespoons unsalted
butter or margarine,
room temperature
1 green onion, cut into
2-inch pieces
2 large eggs
3 tablespoons heavy
cream
1 teaspoon lemon juice
½ teaspoon grated
nutmeg
½ teaspoon ground
coriander
½ teaspoon dill
Salt and freshly ground
black pepper to taste
Lemon slices or chopped
parsley for garnish

Processor

1. Preheat oven to 350° F. Grease six ½-cup
   ovenproof souffle dishes or custard cups.
2. Place brussels sprouts in ½ cup boiling
   water and cook until very soft, about 20
   minutes. Drain.
3. Insert metal blade. Process brussels sprouts
   and butter for 30 seconds, stopping once
   to scrape down the work bowl. You should
   have about 1 cup of puree. Add all remaining ingredients and process for 20 to 30
   seconds. Adjust seasonings.
4. Divide mixture among the dishes and place
   in a large baking pan that will allow 1-inch
   space between them. Pour hot water carefully into the pan, to one-half the height
   of the dishes. Bake for 30 minutes or until
   the puree is firm.
5. Remove the dishes from the pan and let
   rest 10 minutes. Insert a knife gently
   around the edge of each dish and invert
   to unmold. Garnish with lemon slices or
   chopped parsley.

Serves 6

Carrot Puree

5 medium carrots, peeled
and cut into 1-inch
pieces
1 tablespoon butter or
margarine
½ teaspoon nutmeg
1 tablespoon orange juice

*These add a nice texture and color to the plate,
and are just a little different.*

Processor/Microwave

1. Insert metal blade. Chop carrots about 10
   seconds until finely chopped. Remove to
   a microwave-safe baking dish, add 2 tablespoons water, and cover with vented plastic wrap. Cook on high setting until tender,
   about 8 minutes.
2. Place in work bowl with remaining ingredients. Process with 1 or 2 pulses until
   pureed.

Serves 4

Carrot and Sweet Potato Tzimmes

1 bunch carrots, scraped
6 large sweet potatoes, peeled
½ cup pitted prunes
¼ to ½ cup beef stock or orange juice
¼ to ½ cup honey
¼ teaspoon cinnamon
⅛ to ¼ cup chicken fat or margarine

1. Preheat oven to 350° F.

2. Cut carrots into 1-inch slices; cut sweet potatoes into pieces about the same size as the carrots. Boil in salted water to cover until tender but still firm; drain. Place in a casserole with remaining ingredients. Stir gently to combine.

3. Cover and bake for 30 minutes. Stir gently and bake, uncovered, for another 10 minutes.

Serves 8

Carrot-Sweet Potato Pudding

4 medium carrots
2 small sweet potatoes
3 eggs, separated
1 stick (½ cup) butter or margarine, cut into 8 pieces
½ cup soup nut crumbs
½ cup raisins
¾ cup pecans (divided)
¼ cup honey
¼ cup sugar
Juice and peel of 1 large lemon
1 teaspoon cinnamon
½ teaspoon nutmeg

Processor

1. Preheat oven to 375° F. Grease a 1-quart souffle dish.

2. Insert grater blade. Cut carrots and potatoes to fit the feed tube. Grate, and remove from bowl.

3. Change to metal blade. Return carrots and potatoes to work bowl and add egg yolks, butter, soup nut crumbs, raisins, ½ cup pecans, honey, sugar, lemon juice and peel, cinnamon, and nutmeg; mix well with 3 or 4 pulses.

4. Beat egg whites until stiff. Fold into carrot mixture and pour into souffle dish. Sprinkle top with ¼ cup pecans. Bake for 40 minutes.

Serves 6

Glazed Sweet Potatoes

6 medium sweet potatoes
1 cup granulated sugar
½ cup brown sugar
1 tablespoon potato starch
½ teaspoon nutmeg
4 tablespoons butter or margarine
2 teaspoons lemon juice
1 teaspoon vanilla (see conversion table)

Conventional

1. Preheat oven to 350°F. Grease a large baking dish.

2. Wash potatoes and place in a 3-quart saucepan with 1 cup water, and bring to a boil. Cover, turn heat to simmer, and cook 25 to 30 minutes or until soft when pierced with the tip of a knife. Drain. Remove skins and slice the potatoes lengthwise. Place in baking dish.

3. Combine the sugars, potato starch, nutmeg, butter, lemon juice, and vanilla with ½ cup water in a small saucepan. Boil for 2 minutes, stirring constantly. Pour over the potatoes and bake for 45 minutes.

Microwave

In step 2, combine sugars, potato starch, and nutmeg in a 4-cup microwave-safe baking dish with ½ cup water. Cook on high setting for 3 minutes. Stir, and add butter, lemon juice, and vanilla. Microwave on roast setting for 3 minutes or until boiling. Pour over potatoes, cover with vented plastic wrap, and microwave on reheat setting for 7 to 8 minutes. Let stand covered 3 minutes before serving.

Serves 6

Sweet Potato Souffle

6 medium sweet potatoes,
  cooked and peeled
3 eggs, separated
½ cup sugar
½ cup orange juice
2 teaspoons cinnamon
¼ teaspoon nutmeg
¼ teaspoon ground
  cloves

Processor

1 Preheat oven to 400°F. Grease a 2-quart souffle dish.

2. Insert plastic blade. Cut potatoes into quarters and place in work bowl; chop with 4 or 5 quick pulses. Stir with rubber spatula to push the larger chunks down toward the bottom of the bowl.

3. Add egg yolks, sugar, orange juice, and spices. Process 15 to 20 seconds, scraping down sides of bowl once or twice. The potatoes should be smooth and free of lumps. Remove to a large bowl.

4. Beat egg whites until stiff. Fold into the potato mixture. Turn into souffle dish and bake for 30 minutes.

Conventional

Follow processor instructions, mashing the potatoes by hand until very smooth, and beating the egg yolks and remaining ingredients with rotary or electric mixer.

Serves 8 to 10

Boiled New Potatoes with Sour Cream and Chives

1 small clove garlic
2 tablespoons oil
¼ cup fresh parsley
1 tablespoon snipped
  chives
Peel from 1 lemon
6 new potatoes with skins
  on, cut into ½-inch
  cubes
½ teaspoon salt
¼ teaspoon ground
  pepper
½ cup sour cream

Processor/Microwave

1. Insert metal blade in food processor. With machine running, drop garlic through feed tube and mince well. Place in a 2-quart microwave-safe baking dish, add oil, and microwave, uncovered, on high setting for 1 minute.

2. Place parsley, chives, and lemon peel in work bowl and mince with 3 or 4 pulses. Add to casserole with potatoes, salt, and pepper. Cover with vented plastic wrap and microwave on high setting for 9 minutes, stirring every 3 minutes.

3. Stir in sour cream. Cover with vented plastic wrap and microwave on medium setting for 3 minutes or until potatoes are tender. Remove from oven and let stand covered for 2 minutes.

Conventional

Mince garlic, parsley, chives, and lemon peel with a sharp knife. Cook potatoes in ¼ cup water until soft (about 10 minutes). Drain, and season with salt and pepper. Add remaining ingredients. Spoon into a 1-quart greased casserole and bake in a 425° oven for 15 minutes.

Serves 4

Potato Pancakes

6 medium potatoes,
  peeled
1 small onion, cut in half
2 eggs
2 tablespoons Passover
  pancake mix
1 teaspoon salt
Dash of white pepper
¾ cup oil (approx.)

These are delicious served with applesauce or sour cream and chives.

Processor

1. Insert grater blade. Grate the potatoes with very light pressure. Place in a colander and rinse under cold water to remove the starch. Set aside.

2. Change to metal blade. Place onion, eggs, pancake mix, salt, and pepper in work bowl and process for 15 seconds. Add 1 cup of grated potatoes and process for 20 seconds more. Pour this mixture into the remaining grated potatoes and mix well.

3. Pour oil to about ⅛ inch deep in a large skillet over medium-high heat. When oil is hot, drop a large tablespoon of potato mixture into the pan. Flatten to form a pancake, and brown on each side, turning only once. Keep the oil at even heat, adding more if necessary. Drain on paper towels and serve immediately.*

Conventional

Follow processor directions, grating the potatoes and onion by hand.

Makes about 24

*If you are going to freeze the pancakes, do not drain the grease from them. Arrange in a single layer on a cookie sheet, and place in freezer. After 1 hour, you can transfer the pancakes to a plastic bag. Reheat frozen potato pancakes on a cookie sheet for 15 minutes in a 425° oven.

Potato Puffs

2 cups mashed potatoes
  (made from 5 or 6
  potatoes)
3 eggs, separated
½ teaspoon salt
Dash of white pepper
1 tablespoon butter,
  margarine, or chicken
  fat
1 small onion, minced
Paprika

1. Preheat oven to 400°F. Grease muffin tins or a souffle dish very well.

2. Combine mashed potatoes, egg yolks, salt, and pepper. (If you are doing this step in the food processor, use the plastic blade and process for about 15 seconds.) Set aside.

3. Heat butter in a small skillet. Saute onion until golden; do not let it brown. Add to potatoes.

4. Beat egg whites until stiff. Fold into potatoes. Spoon into muffin tins and sprinkle with paprika. Bake about 30 minutes or until golden brown.

Makes 12 to 16 puffs

Roasted Potatoes

See Seder Menu #1 for recipe.

Asparagus with Lemon Sauce

See Seder Menu #1 for recipe.

Brussels Sprouts with Mock Hollandaise Sauce

See Seder Menu #2 for recipe.

Sauces

Hollandaise Sauce

1 stick (½ cup) butter or margarine
4 egg yolks
3 teaspoons lemon juice
½ teaspoon salt

Place butter in a double boiler. Add egg yolks, lemon juice, salt, and ½ cup water. Cook over hot water, beating constantly with a wire whisk until thick. Makes 1 cup.

Note: You may make this a little ahead of time. When you are ready to use, reheat over hot water. If sauce begins to separate, add a teaspoon of butter or margarine and beat until the sauce is smooth.

Easy Hollandaise

1 stick (½ cup) unsalted butter or margarine
4 egg yolks
Juice of 2 lemons
1 teaspoon oil

Serve over any green vegetable, poached fish, or open-faced hot sandwich.

Place all ingredients in a double boiler. Cook over hot water, stirring constantly, until thickened. Makes 1 cup.

Mock Hollandaise Sauce

See Seder Menu #2 for recipe.

Horseradish Sauce

See Seder Menu #2 for recipe.

Mayonnaise Sauce

3 heaping tablespoons
  mayonnaise
Juice of ½ lemon
1½ teaspoons sugar
Salt, pepper, red pepper,
  and paprika to taste
Cream or non-dairy
  creamer

Serve over cold vegetables or fish.

Combine mayonnaise, lemon juice, sugar, and seasonings, and mix well. Add cream slowly until the sauce is the consistency you like. Makes ½ cup.

Fresh Lemon Sauce

1 tablespoon potato
  starch
1 cup sugar
Juice and grated peel of 1
  lemon
2 tablespoons butter or
  margarine

You can serve this sauce cold over salads or warm over vegetables.

1. Combine potato starch and sugar in a 1-quart saucepan. Gradually stir in 2 cups hot water. Cook over medium heat, stirring until thickened.

2. Add the lemon juice, lemon peel, and butter. Cook 1 minute longer. Remove from heat and let cool. Refrigerate. Makes 2¼ cups.

Main Dishes

Eggs & Cheese

Macaroni and Cheese, Passover Style

3 large eggs
3 ½ cups matzah farfel
(or 6 matzahs, broken
up)
½ pound cheddar cheese
1 cup milk or half-and-
half
1 teaspoon salt
¼ teaspoon white pepper
1 pint sour cream
1 stick (½ cup) butter,
cut into 16 pieces

For a slimmer version, use skim milk and cut down on the butter.

1. Preheat oven to 350°F. Grease a 2-quart casserole with butter.

2. Beat 2 eggs well with a wire whisk and pour over farfel. Cut up cheese into small pieces.

3. Beat remaining egg with a wire whisk, and stir in milk, salt, and pepper.

4. Layer in casserole as follows: matzah farfel, half the cheese, half the sour cream (in dabs), half the butter. Distribute each layer evenly. Pour the milk mixture over the top. Cover and bake for 30 minutes. Remove cover and bake 10 to 15 minutes to brown. Cut into squares.

Serves 6 to 8

DIAGRAM FOR BLINTZES

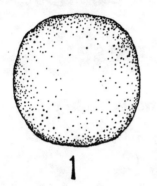

1

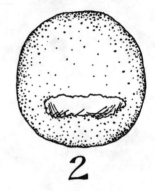

2

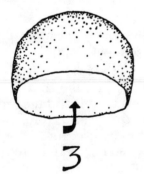

3

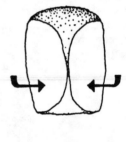

4

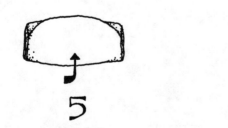

5

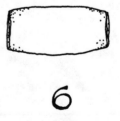

6

Cheese Blintzes

Batter
3 eggs
½ teaspoon salt
¾ cup matzah cake meal
1 teaspoon butter
1 ½ cups milk
Melted butter or
  margarine for frying

Sweet Cheese Filling
8-ounce carton cottage
  cheese
7 ½-ounce package
  farmers cheese
1 egg
½ teaspoon sugar
½ teaspoon cinnamon
¼ teaspoon nutmeg
¼ cup white raisins

Processor

1. Insert metal blade. Place all batter ingredient in work bowl, and process for 10 to 15 seconds. *Do not double the recipe or you might have leakage from your work bowl.* Transfer to bowl or pitcher and refrigerate for 1 hour.

2. Process filling ingredients together for 10 to 15 seconds, scraping sides of bowl as necessary. Place in refrigerator while making crepes.

3. Heat a 6-inch frying pan on medium-high heat. Brush lightly with melted butter. Pour in just enough batter to cover the bottom of the pan, pouring excess back into container. Fry on *one side only* for 30 to 40 seconds, until no moisture remains on top of the crepe. Turn out on a board covered with a clean towel, rapping bottom of pan to loosen if necessary. Repeat until all the batter is used up.

4. For each blintz, place about 1 tablespoon of filling on the browned side, halfway between the center and the edge. Fold the bottom and side edges of the crepe over the filling, then roll away from you like a jelly roll.*

5. Heat butter in a large skillet, and brown blintzes over medium-high heat until golden. Serve with sour cream, cinnamon-sugar, or preserves.

Conventional

In steps 1 and 2, use a blender or electric mixer.

Makes 16 to 18 blintzes; serves 6 to 8

*You may freeze blintzes at this point. Bake frozen blintzes in a 350° oven for 15 to 20 minutes *Do not defrost first.*

Matzah Brie (Fried Matzahs)

4 matzos
3 eggs, lightly beaten
2 tablespoons butter

Break up matzos and place in a colander. Pour boiling water over. Mix into beaten eggs, stirring until egg is slightly absorbed. Heat butter in a skillet, pour in matzos, and cook until golden. Turn and cook other side. May cook as a single layer or break up as desired.

Serves 4

Hoppel Poppel

4 medium potatoes, cooked (3 cups sliced)
1 medium onion
8 eggs
8 thin slices salami
½ cup non-dairy creamer
1 tablespoon fresh parsley
1 tablespoon fresh chopped chives
1 teaspoon salt
½ teaspoon paprika
¼ teaspoon pepper
¼ cup pareve margarine

Be careful not to overstir when you cook the eggs. This dish is much better served with the eggs a little underdone, because the retained heat completes the cooking.

Processor

1. Insert slicing blade. Slice potatoes and onion and set aside.

2. Change to metal blade and process remaining ingredients (except margarine) for 30 seconds, in two batches. Set aside.

3. Melt margarine over medium-high heat in a large skillet. Add potatoes and onions. Cook, stirring occasionally, until potatoes begin to brown and onion is tender, about 5 to 7 minutes.

4. Reduce heat to medium and add egg mixture. As eggs begin to set, gently draw a pancake turner across bottom and sides of skillet, forming large soft curds. Continue until the eggs are thickened.

Conventional

Follow processor instructions, slicing and chopping the vegetables by hand.

Serves 4 to 6

Pineapple Upside-Down Kugel

6 large eggs
¼ cup milk
5 egg matzahs
¼ cup butter or
  margarine, softened
¾ cup brown sugar
  (divided)
8 slices canned
  pineapple, well drained
¼ cup melted butter or
  margarine
½ teaspoon salt
½ teaspoon cinnamon
Pinch of ginger
Juice and grated peel of 1
  lemon
½ cup chopped nuts
½ cup chopped dried
  fruits (apricots,
  peaches, pears)
½ cup raisins

Processor

1. Preheat oven to 350°F. Beat 3 eggs and combine with milk. Break matzahs into small pieces and soak in this mixture.

2. Grease a 9-inch square or 2-quart baking pan with ¼ cup butter, and sprinkle with ¼ cup brown sugar. Cut pineapple slices in half and place on sugar.

3. Insert metal blade. Place 3 eggs, melted butter, ½ cup sugar, salt, cinnamon, ginger, lemon juice, and lemon peel in work bowl. Process for 15 seconds, scraping down sides as necessary. Add nuts and matzah mixture. Pulse 1 or 2 times. Remove to a bowl.

4. Fold in chopped dried fruit and raisins. Transfer to baking pan, and bake 45 to 50 minutes, until set and golden brown. Let stand 5 minutes; loosen all around with spatula and invert over serving dish

Conventional

In step 3, beat 3 eggs, melted margarine, ½ cup sugar, salt, cinnamon, ginger, lemon juice, and grated rind with an electric mixer.

Serves 6 to 8

Apple-Nut Kugel

4 matzahs
½ cup water or milk
3 eggs
½ cup sugar
¼ cup melted butter or
   margarine
1 teaspoon cinnamon
¼ teaspoon salt
2 large tart apples,
   peeled, cored, and
   sliced
1 cup walnuts, chopped
½ cup white raisins
1 tablespoon butter or
   margarine

1. Preheat oven to 350°F. Grease a 9-inch square pan. Break matzah into small pieces and soak in water or milk until soft. Drain well.

2. Combine eggs, sugar, melted butter, cinnamon, and salt and beat with a wire whisk. Pour over drained matzah. Stir in apples, walnuts, and raisins. Pour into baking pan, and dot with butter. Bake 30 to 45 minutes or until slightly brown.

Serves 8 to 10

Matzah Kugel with White Wine Sauce

6 matzahs
6 eggs, separated
½ cup sugar
1 teaspoon vanilla (see conversion table)
1 teaspoon grated lemon peel
1 tablespoon lemon juice
4 tart apples
½ cup dark raisins
½ cup white raisins
1 cup slivered almonds
4 tablespoons butter or margarine
Confectioners' sugar (see conversion table)

The wine sauce may be served hot or cold, and it will keep in the refrigerator up to 24 hours.

1. Preheat oven to 350°F. Grease a 2-quart casserole. Break matzahs into small pieces and soak in water until soft.

2. Beat egg whites until stiff but not dry. Set aside. Beat egg yolks until thick and lemon-colored, about 5 minutes. Add sugar, vanilla, lemon peel, and lemon juice.

3. Peel and core apples, and cut into small pieces.

4. Drain matzahs and squeeze out the excess water. Fold into egg yolk mixture along with apples, raisins, and almonds. Gently fold egg whites into egg yolk mixture.

5. Place in casserole. Cut butter into small pieces and distribute over top. Bake 45 to 50 minutes or until nicely browned.

6. To serve, invert on a platter and dust with confectioners' sugar. Serve with White Wine Sauce.

Serves 8 to 10

White Wine Sauce

6 egg yolks (freeze whites for later use)
¾ cup sugar
1 cup dry white wine
2 teaspoons potato starch

1. Using a wire whisk or portable electric mixer, beat egg yolks in top of double boiler (off heat), adding sugar ¼ cup at a time. When sugar is blended in, gradually beat in wine and potato starch.

2. Place over boiling water, stirring continuously with wooden spoon, until mixture begins to thicken (about 10 minutes). Makes about 2 cups.

Asparagus-Cheese Casserole

1 cup soup nut crumbs
1 stick (½ cup) butter or margarine
4 ounces sharp cheddar cheese, grated
2 tablespoons butter or margarine
1 ½ tablespoons potato starch
1 ½ cups milk
Salt and pepper to taste
1 pound fresh asparagus, cooked (may substitute canned asparagus)
½ cup slivered almonds, or more to taste

Conventional

1. Using the processor (metal blade) or a pastry blender, mix the crumbs with 1 stick of butter. Combine with grated cheese.

2. Melt 2 tablespoons of butter in a saucepan. Blend in the potato starch with a wire whisk until smooth, then blend in the milk. Cook, stirring constantly, until thickened, 3 to 4 minutes. Season with salt and pepper.

3. Preheat oven to 350°. Layer in an open casserole as follows: ½ cup cheese mixture, asparagus, almonds, ½ cup sauce; end with a layer of nuts on top. You may want to add extra almonds. Bake for 20 minutes.

Microwave

In step 2, you can make the sauce in the microwave. Melt the butter in a 2-cup microwave-safe measuring cup on medium for 1 minute. Blend in the potato starch with a wire whisk until smooth, then blend in the milk. Cook on medium setting for 4 minutes; stir and cook 3 to 4 minutes longer. Stir in salt and pepper.

Serves 8 to 10

Broccoli Souffle

1 large head broccoli
1 small onion, cut in half
2 eggs
10-ounce can mushroom soup
⅓ cup mayonnaise
1 tablespoon lemon juice
½ cup cashews
6 ounces sharp cheddar cheese (about ½ c. grated)
6 ounces mozzarella cheese (about ½ c. grated)

Processor

1. Insert metal blade. Cut the broccoli into 2-inch pieces. Place in work bowl with onion, and chop with 3 pulses. For the microwave, place in a 2-quart microwave-safe baking dish, add ⅓ cup water, and cover with vented plastic wrap; cook on high setting for 6 to 8 minutes. For stovetop, cook until tender in a large saucepan. Drain.

2. Place eggs, soup, mayonnaise, and lemon juice in work bowl and pulse 3 to 4 times. Add the cashews and process for 5 seconds. Set aside.

3. Change to grater blade and grate the cheeses.

4. Preheat the oven to 350°. Grease a 2-quart casserole.

5. Fold the soup mixture and half the grated cheese into the cooked broccoli. Transfer to the casserole and sprinkle with the remaining cheese. Bake for 40 minutes.

Conventional

Follow processor instructions, chopping the broccoli, onion, and nuts by hand. Shred the cheese.

Serves 6

Eggplant Lasagna

1 medium eggplant,
  unpeeled
½ pound fresh
  mushrooms
2 onions (1 red, 1 yellow)
2 large cloves garlic
½ cup oil for sauteing
½ teaspoon fresh
  oregano (or ¼ tsp.
  dried)
¼ teaspoon fresh thyme
  (or ⅛ tsp. dried)
16 ounces mozzarella
  cheese (2 cups)
12 ounces parmesan
  cheese (1½ cups)
8 ounces farmers cheese
4 matzahs
1½ cups dry red wine
24 ounces tomato sauce
  (see conversion table)

Processor

1. Insert slicing blade. Cut eggplant to fit feed tube. Slice eggplant and mushrooms, and set aside.

2. Insert metal blade. Chop onions and garlic. Set aside.

3. Heat oil in a large frying pan, and saute eggplant, mushrooms, onions, and garlic until soft. Add oregano and thyme and saute 2 to 3 minutes. Set aside.

4. Chop parmesan with metal blade until fine. Change to grater blade and grate mozzarella. Break up farmers cheese and set aside.

5. Preheat the oven to 350°F. Soak the matzahs ½ minute in the red wine.

6. Make 2 layers in a 9 x 13 open casserole as follows: tomato sauce, sauteed vegetables, matzahs, cheese; end with sauce as top layer. Bake 45 to 50 minutes. Let stand for 10 minutes before serving.

Conventional

Follow processer instructions, chopping vegetables and grating cheeses by hand.

Serves 8 to 10

Eggplant Casserole

1 small eggplant, peeled
 and sliced
1 medium zucchini
3 small tomatoes, cut in
 half
1 medium onion, cut in
 quarters
1 large clove garlic
1 medium green pepper
½ pound mushrooms
6 ounces mozzarella
 cheese (about ½ c.)
6 ounces parmesan
 cheese (about ½ c.)
1 tablespoon oil
1 teaspoon chopped fresh
 basil (or ½ tsp. dried)
1 teaspoon fresh thyme
 (or ½ tsp. dried)
1 tablespoon potato
 starch
2 cups tomato sauce (see
 conversion table)
½ cup dry red wine
Salt and pepper to taste

Processor

1. Place eggplant in a 1-quart microwave-safe baking dish with ¼ cup water; cover with vented plastic wrap, and microwave on high setting for 10 minutes. Or cook in a small amount of water in a covered saucepan until soft.

2. Preheat the oven to 350°F. Grease a 9 x 13 baking dish.

3. Insert slicing blade and slice the zucchini, then the tomatoes, using light pressure. Set aside.

4. Change to metal blade. With machine running, drop onion and garlic through the feed tube. Insert slicing blade and slice green pepper and mushrooms. Set aside.

5. Insert grater blade and grate the cheeses. Set aside.

6. Heat oil in a large frying pan, and saute onion, garlic, green pepper, and mushrooms over medium-high heat with basil and thyme for 5 minutes, until soft but not brown. Combine potato starch, tomato sauce, and wine, and pour over the sauteed vegetables. Heat for 1 or 2 minutes, stirring well. Season with salt and pepper.

7. Fill the baking pan in 2 layers as follows: eggplant, zucchini, tomatoes, sauteed vegetables, and cheese. Bake, uncovered, for 40 minutes. Let rest for 10 minutes before slicing.

Conventional

Follow processor directions, slicing and chopping vegetables with a sharp knife, and shredding cheese by hand.

Serves 8

Zucchini Souffle

4 to 6 zucchini, sliced
3 eggs
1 cup sour cream
6 ounces cheddar cheese, cubed or shredded
6 ounces mozzarella cheese, cubed or shredded
1 small onion, minced
1 small clove garlic, minced
½ teaspoon salt
Dash of pepper
Dash of paprika

Processor

1. Place zucchini in a saucepan with ½ cup boiling water. Cook for 15 minutes. Drain.
2. Insert metal blade. Place zucchini in work bowl and pulse until mashed. Place in the bottom of a 10-inch greased casserole.
2. Add eggs, and sour cream to the work bowl and process for 3 seconds. Add all other ingredients, reserving ¼ cup of mozzarella cheese. Blend with 3 or 4 pulses, scraping sides of bowl as necessary, until smooth. Pour over the zucchini and sprinkle with remaining ¼ cup of mozzarella. Refrigerate at least 6 hours or overnight.
3. Bake in a preheated 350° oven for 30 to 45 minutes or until the top is golden brown and puffy. Serve immediately.

Serves 6

Note: You may want to add ¼ cup cooked rice to the casserole along with the zucchini in step 2. Sephardic Jews eat rice on Passover.

Spinach-Rice Casserole

2 packages (10 oz. each) frozen spinach
2 medium onions, chopped
1 stick (½ cup) butter or margarine
1 cup cooked rice*
Salt and pepper to taste
5-ounce can evaporated milk
½ cup heavy cream
8 ounces sharp cheddar cheese (about 2 cups), grated

1. Cook spinach according to directions on package. Drain and chop. Preheat oven to 325°F.
2. Heat the butter in a frying pan and saute the onions until golden. Add spinach and rice. Season with salt and pepper. Cook for 3 or 4 minutes.
3. Remove pan from heat and stir in milk, cream, and 1 ½ cups of cheese. Place in a 2-quart casserole. Cover with remaining cheese and bake for 30 minutes.

Serves 10

* Sephardic Jews may eat rice on Passover.

Fish

Poached Fish Fillets with Herb Sauce

6 six-ounce fish fillets
(salmon, cod, halibut)
Salt and pepper to taste
1 bay leaf
1 lemon, sliced
1 leek (white part only),
chopped
1 teaspoon fresh thyme,
chopped
½ cup chopped fresh
parsley leaves
1 clove garlic, chopped
1 cup dry white wine
2 tablespoons butter
2 tablespoons potato
starch
1 teaspoon chopped fresh
basil
1 teaspoon dried oregano
¼ cup mayonnaise
Pimento for garnish

1. Wash fish fillets in cold water. Dry with paper towels. Season with salt and pepper, and place in a 9 x 14 baking dish. Add the bay leaf and lemon slices.

2. Preheat oven to 450°F.

3. Combine the chopped leek, thyme, parsley, and garlic with the wine in a small saucepan. Bring to a boil, and pour over the fillets. Cut 1 tablespoon of butter into small pieces and distribute evenly over the top. Cover with aluminum foil that has been greased with the remaining butter. Bake for no more than 30 minutes. (Allow 8 minutes per pound if fillets are thick and 5 or 6 minutes per pound if they are thin.) Remove bay leaf and lemon slices.

4. Drain liquid from baking dish into a bowl. Add potato starch, basil, and oregano; mix with a wire whisk. Fold in mayonnaise. Spoon 1 tablespoon of sauce over each fillet. Garnish with pimento, and serve with the remaining sauce on the side.

Serves 6

Fish Fillets with Yogurt

6 fish fillets (scrod, cod, salmon, or halibut)—about 2 pounds
Salt and freshly ground pepper to taste
2 large eggs
¼ cup potato starch
¼ cup matzah cake meal
½ stick (¼ lb.) unsalted butter
¼ cup oil
8-ounce carton plain yogurt
2 tablespoons chopped fresh dill
1 green onion, chopped
Chopped parsley for garnish

1. Preheat oven to 350°F. Season the fillets with salt and pepper. Beat the eggs. Sift the potato starch and cake meal into a small bowl.

2. Heat the butter and oil in a large skillet over moderately high heat. Dip the fillets in the beaten egg and then in the sifted meal to coat. Saute until well browned, about 1 minute on each side.

3. Remove with a slotted turner to a baking dish. Arrange the fillets side by side in one layer. Combine yogurt, dill, and green onion and spoon evenly over the fillets.

4. Bake in the center of the oven for 15 minutes or until the thickest part of the fish flakes easily. Garnish with chopped parsley.

Serves 6

Salmon Fillets for Two

2 eight-ounce salmon fillets
¼ cup white wine
2 tablespoons mayonnaise
1 teaspoon grated parmesan cheese

Conventional

1. Preheat oven to 450°F.

2. Wash salmon and dry with paper towels. Place in a small baking dish. Combine wine, mayonnaise, and cheese; spread on the salmon. Bake, covered, for 10 minutes.

Microwave

In step 2, place fish on a microwave-safe pie plate, cover with vented plastic wrap, and cook on high setting for 6 minutes.

Serves 2

Fresh Lake Trout Baked in Wine

5- to 6-pound lake trout, boned
Lemon juice
1 tablespoon chopped shallots
½ teaspoon dried thyme
¼ teaspoon kosher salt
Dash of white pepper
1 cup dry white wine
1 stick (½ cup) butter, cut into small pieces
½ cup cream or milk (approx.)
1 tablespoon butter
1 teaspoon potato starch
¼ cup grated cheese (swiss, cheddar, or parmesan)

1. Preheat oven to 325°F. Dip the fish in lemon juice mixed with cold water. Dry well with paper towels. Place in baking dish.

2. Sprinkle with shallots, thyme, salt, and pepper. Add wine. Distribute pieces of butter evenly over the fish.

3. Bake, covered, for 15 to 20 minutes, or until fish flakes and feels firm to the touch. Remove from oven.

4. Pour liquid from pan into 2-cup measuring cup. Add cream to make 2 cups.

5. Melt 1 tablespoon butter in saucepan, add potato starch, and stir well with wire whisk. When mixture begins to bubble, add cream mixture and cheese. Continue stirring until it thickens. Pour over fish and serve. (For a better color, place under broiler for a minute or two.)

Serves 10 to 12

Boston Scrod with Vegetables and White Wine

¼ cup mayonnaise
Juice of 1 lemon
8 six-ounce Boston scrod fillets
¾ cup oil
¼ cup fresh chopped parsley
3 medium shallots, chopped
2 stalks celery, chopped
1 small green pepper, chopped
1 large leek, chopped
3 medium tomatoes, peeled, seeded, and chopped
2 cloves garlic, minced (optional)
2 teaspoons fresh thyme, chopped
4 tablespoons butter
½ cup dry white wine

1. Preheat oven to 500°F. Combine mayonnaise and lemon juice. Spread evenly over the fillets. Place in a 9 x 14 baking dish.

2. Brown in oven for 10 minutes. Remove from oven and let rest. (The dish may be prepared up to this point and finished later.)

3. Pour oil into a large skillet. Saute the parsley, shallots, celery, green pepper, and leek for 5 minutes. Add tomatoes, garlic, and thyme and continue cooking for 5 minutes.

4. Set oven to 350°. Place some of the sauteed vegetables on each fillet. Top each with ½ teaspoon butter. Pour wine over the top and bake for 10 minutes or until fish flakes easily.

Serves 8

Baked Stuffed Whitefish

3- to 4-pound whitefish
1 tablespoon butter
Juice of 1 lemon
½ cup white wine
½ cup shredded swiss
cheese
1 lemon, sliced thin

Stuffing

¼ cup butter or
margarine
1 green pepper, minced
2 shallots or green
onions, minced
2 stalks celery, minced
¼ cup parsley, chopped
2 tomatoes, chopped
¼ cup white wine
¼ cup soup nut crumbs
¼ teaspoon oregano
Salt and pepper to taste

Allow ½ pound per serving for fresh fish. When baking fish, measure the fish at the thickest point and allow 10 minutes for each inch of thickness.

1. Wash fish in cold water. Pat dry. Cut slits in skin on top side of fish in 3 or 4 places. Preheat oven to 450°F.

2. Combine butter, lemon juice, and wine in small saucepan and heat. (For microwave, place in 2-quart measure and cook on high setting for 2 minutes.) Rub fish inside and out with mixture and put into a large baking dish.

3. Make stuffing. Heat butter in skillet and saute minced green pepper, shallots, and celery for 2 or 3 minutes. Add chopped parsley and tomatoes and cook about 2 minutes longer. Add wine, crumbs, and oregano and mix well. Season with salt and pepper.

4. Stuff cavity of fish and fasten with skewers. Place in baking dish and surround with lemon slices. Bake about 30 minutes, or until the thickest part of the fish flakes easily.

5. Cover with cheese and place under broiler until cheese begins to bubble. Remove skewers, slice, and serve.

Serves 6 to 8

Baked Gefilte Fish Loaf

2 pounds fish fillets
(mixed whitefish and
pike)
2 onions, cut in quarters
1 carrot, cut into 2-inch
pieces
2 eggs
½ cup water
1 tablespoon sugar
1 teaspoon oil
½ teaspoon salt
¼ teaspoon white pepper
1 green pepper, sliced
into rings

Processor

1. Preheat oven to 350°F. Grease a microwave-safe loaf pan (8 x 4 x 3) with melted butter.

2. Insert metal blade. Cut up fish and place in work bowl; process for 20 seconds. Add onions and carrot, and process 25 to 30 seconds. Add eggs, water, sugar, oil, salt, and pepper; process for 15 seconds, scraping down sides of bowl as necessary.

3. Place green pepper rings on bottom of pan and spread with fish mixture. Bake uncovered 45 minutes to 1 hour. Remove loaf from pan by turning upside down over a platter. Serve hot or cold.

Serves 6 to 8

Fresh Fish Croquettes

1 medium onion
½ stalk celery
1 carrot
1 pound fish fillets (sole,
haddock, or perch), cut
into 2-inch pieces
2 eggs
Pinch of thyme
½ cup soup nut crumbs
¼ cup chopped fresh
parsley
1 teaspoon salt
Freshly ground pepper
Oil for frying

These freeze very well. To make a double recipe, process in two separate batches.

Processor

1. Insert metal blade. Cut onion, celery, and carrot into chunks. Process until minced, about 6 to 8 seconds. Add fish, eggs, and thyme to work bowl and process for 20 seconds or until fish is minced. Add crumbs, parsley, salt, and pepper. Process with 2 or 3 pulses until mixed. Remove to mixing bowl.

2. Wet hands with water and form into 6 croquettes.

3. Heat oil over medium heat and brown croquettes on all sides until golden brown. Drain on paper towels.

Serves 4

Meat and Poultry

Brisket

4 to 4½ pounds brisket
1 large onion, cut in
   quarters
4 cloves garlic
¼ cup fresh parsley
2 stalks celery with leaves
2 large carrots
1 bay leaf
8 ounces tomato sauce
   (see conversion table)
1 cup dry red wine
1 cube beef bouillion
1 tablespoon salt
¼ teaspoon white pepper
1 tablespoon beef broth
   mix
1 tablespoon potato
   starch

This is my family's favorite brisket recipe, and I make it for most of the holidays. It is easy, very traditional, and serves a few or a crowd. It may be made ahead and it freezes well.

Processor

1. Preheat oven to 300° F. Wash brisket in cold water and dry with paper towels. Place on a rack in a large roasting pan.

2. Insert metal blade. Place onion, garlic, and parsley in work bowl and chop for 5 seconds. Distribute over brisket. Place celery stalks, carrots, and bay leaf around the brisket.

3. Process tomato sauce, wine, bouillion cube, salt, pepper, and beef broth mix for 30 seconds, and pour over brisket.

4. Cover, and roast for 45 minutes to 1 hour per pound. Check for doneness by sticking with a fork. It should be tender but not extremely soft. Remove from oven and separate the meat from the liquid and vegetables. Let cool before slicing.

5. Place half the liquid and vegetables in the work bowl and process for 10 seconds. Repeat with remaining liquid and vegetables and the potato starch.

6. Slice brisket and place in baking dish. Pour gravy over the meat and heat, covered, in a 350° oven for 30 minutes.

Conventional

Chop vegetables with a sharp knife. In step 5, you can use a blender or food mill.

Serves 6

Shoulder Roast

4 to 5 pound shoulder
  roast
½ teaspoon white pepper
2 to 3 onions, thinly
  sliced

This is very easy and tasty! Make sure you get a good prime piece of meat.

1. Preheat oven to 325° F. Rub roast all over with pepper.
2. Place onions in open roasting pan. Set the roast over the onions. Bake, uncovered, 20 minutes to the pound. Cool slightly before slicing.

Serves 8 to 10

Barbecue Sauce

1 small onion, chopped
1 stick (½ cup) margarine
1 cup ketchup
½ cup water
Juice from ½ lemon
2 tablespoons brown
  sugar
1 tablespoon oil
Salt, pepper, paprika to
  taste

This is great for beef barbecue!

Saute onion in margarine. Add remaining ingredients and cook over medium heat for 10 minutes. Makes about 1½ cups

Meat Patties

2 cups cooked meat
  (chicken, roast beef,
  lamb), ground or
  chopped in food
  processor
1 onion, minced
2 eggs
½ cup matzah meal
Seasonings of your choice
  (rosemary, garlic,
  chives, basil)
Salt and white pepper to
  taste
3 tablespoons oil

These make a nice luncheon dish. They may be made ahead and frozen, then reheated in a hot oven or microwave.

1. Combine meat, onion, eggs, and matzah meal. Mix until well blended. Season to taste, and shape into patties.
2. Heat oil in a skillet on medium-high heat. Brown patties a few minutes on each side.

Serves 4

Meat Blintzes

Batter

3 large eggs
½ cup matzah cake meal
1 cup water or broth
¼ teaspoon salt
1 teaspoon chicken fat, optional
Oil for frying

Filling

3 cups cooked leftover meat or chicken, cut in ½-inch chunks
1 small cooked potato, cut in quarters
1 medium onion, cut in quarters
½ cup matzah meal
½ teaspoon salt
¼ teaspoon black pepper
1 large egg
¼ cup leftover gravy or broth

Processor

1. Insert metal blade. Place all batter ingredients in work bowl. Process for 10 seconds. Transfer to bowl or pitcher and refrigerate for 1 hour.

2. Process filling ingredients: mince the meat, about 6 to 8 seconds. Add potato, and pulse 1 or 2 times. Add remaining ingredients and process 3 or 4 seconds more. Place in refrigerator while making crepes.

3. Lightly oil a 6-inch frying pan and place on medium-high heat. Pour in just enough batter to cover the bottom of the pan; pour excess back into the container. Fry for 30 to 40 seconds on *one side only*, until no moisture remains on top of the crepe. Turn out on a board covered with a clean towel, rapping bottom of pan to loosen if necessary. Repeat until all the batter is used up.

4. For each blintz, place about 1 tablespoon of filling on the browned side halfway between the center and the edge. Fold the bottom and side edges of the crepe over the filling, then roll away from you like a jelly roll.* (*See Cheese Blintzes recipe for illustration.*)

5. In a large skillet, brown in oil over medium-high heat until golden. Serve with a tasty gravy or homemade chutney.

Conventional

In step 1, use a blender or electric mixer. In step 2, use a meat grinder.

Makes 12 to 14 blintzes; serves 6 to 8

*You may freeze blintzes at this point. Bake frozen blintzes in a 375° oven for 15 minutes. *Do not defrost first.*

DIAGRAM FOR STUFFED CABBAGE

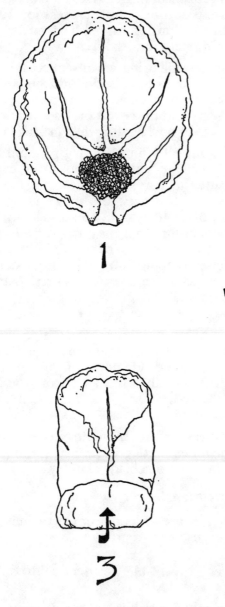

1

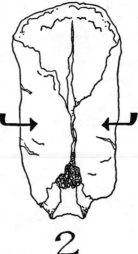

2

3

4

Stuffed Cabbage with Sweet and Sour Sauce

1 green cabbage (about 3 lbs.)
2 pounds lean ground beef
1 medium potato, peeled and grated
1 small onion, chopped
2 large eggs, lightly beaten
½ cup ketchup
½ cup matzah meal
1 bay leaf
Salt and pepper to taste

Sauce

16 ounces tomato sauce (see conversion table)
⅓ cup brown sugar
14-ounce can cranberry sauce
¼ cup plus 1 tablespoon lemon juice

1. Combine all sauce ingredients and mix in blender or food processor with metal blade. Pour into a 4-quart ovenproof stewing pot and let simmer over medium heat while you prepare the cabbage balls.

2. Core the cabbage. Pull off as many leaves as possible until they become too small to hold filling. Bring 1 cup of water to a boil, place the leaves in the water, cover, turn to simmer, and let cook for 10 minutes until soft, or microwave in a 2-quart microwave-safe container with ¼ cup water on high setting for 6 minutes. Drain.

3. Combine ground beef, grated potato, chopped onion, eggs, ketchup, matzah meal, and ½ cup water. Mix well. Season with salt and pepper.

4. Fill the cabbage leaves by placing about 1 tablespoon of the ground meat mixture in the middle of each leaf. Fold over the sides and roll the cabbage ball away from you. Place seam side down in the simmering sauce. Continue until all the cabbage leaves have been used. If you have some ground beef balls left over, just add them to the sauce. Cut up remaining small pieces of cabbage and distribute them evenly over the top of the balls. Add the bay leaf. Check for seasonings. You may wish to add more lemon juice, cranberry sauce, or brown sugar, according to your taste.

5. Simmer, covered, on top of the stove for 20 minutes. Preheat the oven to 350° F. Bake uncovered for 20 minutes more to brown the top.

Serves 8

Note: This dish freezes very well. To reheat, preheat the oven to 300° F and place directly from freezer into the oven. Reheat 30 min. covered, then 30 min. uncovered.

Meat Loaf

1 clove garlic
8 ounces tomato sauce
  (see conversion table)
1 egg
3 green onions, cut in
  2-inch pieces
½ cup mushrooms
½ teaspoon dried
  rosemary
1 teaspoon salt
¼ teaspoon white pepper
½ pound ground beef
½ pound ground veal
¼ cup matzah farfel
¼ cup red wine

Processor

1. Insert metal blade. Mince garlic by dropping through feed tube while machine is running. Add tomato sauce, egg, and green onions to work bowl and process about 6 seconds. Add mushrooms, rosemary, salt, and pepper. Process with 3 or 4 pulses until mushrooms just disappear.

2. Preheat oven to 350°. Soak farfel in red wine for 10 minutes.

3. Combine beef and veal in a large bowl. Add sauce mixture. Add farfel and mix well. Pack lightly in a greased 9 x 5 loaf pan. Bake for 1 hour or until loaf begins to pull away from sides and the top is brown. Let cool slightly before slicing.

Conventional

In step 1, mince garlic and chop vegetables with a sharp knife. Combine with sauce ingredients by hand.

Serves 6

Note: This recipe freezes well and makes wonderful cold sandwiches.

Roasted Lamb

6- to 7-pound lamb
  shoulder roast
Salt and pepper
1 clove garlic, cut in half
Juice of 1 lemon
1 teaspoon fresh
  rosemary (or ⅓ tsp.
  dried)
8 ounces uncooked pine
  nuts

1. Preheat oven to 350° F. Wipe lamb all over with a damp paper towel, then rub well with salt, pepper, and garlic. Sprinkle generously with lemon juice.

2. Using the tip of a sharp knife, make several small slashes in the meat. Insert (or sprinkle with) rosemary.

3. Place in a roasting pan. Roast, uncovered, about 1½ to 2 hours, or about 20 minutes to the pound. Baste and turn frequently so the lamb will cook evenly on all sides. After the first hour, place most of the pine nuts around the meat.

4. Let rest 15 minutes in pan before slicing. Make gravy from the meat drippings and garnish with remaining pine nuts.

Serves 8 to 10

Veal Scallops with Lemon

8 veal scallops, sliced
  very thin
2 eggs
Pinch of salt
¾ cup soup nut crumbs
1 stick (½ cup) pareve
  margarine
½ cup oil
3 tablespoons lemon juice
½ cup chopped parsley
Lemon wedges
Chopped parsley for
  garnish

1. Remove all fat from veal. Beat eggs and salt in a bowl. Place crumbs in a pie plate.

2. Dip each veal scallop in the beaten eggs, making sure it is well coated, then roll in crumbs. Refrigerate for at least 30 minutes (to help the crumbs adhere during cooking).

3. Heat margarine and oil in a frying pan. Saute the scallops for 2 or 3 minutes on each side. Drain on paper towels to absorb excess grease, then place on the serving platter.

4. Cook lemon juice and parsley in a frying pan over very high heat for 1 minute. Pour over scallops. Sprinkle with a little extra chopped parsley for color, and serve with lemon wedges.

Serves 4 to 6

Stuffed Veal Breast

11-pound veal breast
1 tablespoon paprika
2 medium onions, sliced
2 large cloves garlic, cut
  into slivers
1½ cups dry red wine
Veal Gravy (recipe
  follows)

Stuffing

3 sticks (1½ cups) pareve
  margarine
2 medium onions,
  chopped
3 stalks celery, chopped
½ pound fresh
  mushrooms, sliced
7 cups matzah farfel
1 egg
1 tablespoon paprika
1 teaspoon salt
¼ teaspoon pepper
1½ cans (10 oz. each)
  chicken broth

Our rabbi's wife, Vivian Zimmelman, shared this recipe with me. The first time I made it, it was a winner! If you want something different for any occasion, try it. Be sure to ask the butcher to cut a pocket in the veal for you.

1. Rub the veal with the paprika and place in a large roasting pan. Make several slashes in the veal and insert slivers of garlic. Cover with half the onion slices and the remaining garlic. Pour the wine over everything, cover, and refrigerate overnight.

2. Make the stuffing. Heat margarine in medium-hot skillet and saute onions, celery, and mushrooms for 5 to 10 minutes. Add matzah farfel and cook 5 more minutes, stirring occasionally.

3. Beat the egg in a small bowl, then add paprika, salt, pepper, and chicken broth. Use a wire whisk to blend well. Add to the farfel mixture and stir to blend well. Stuff the veal pocket. (If you have extra stuffing, place it in a well-greased casserole and bake covered for 20 minutes and then uncovered for 10 minutes.)

4. Preheat the oven to 325°. Place the remaining sliced onion in a large roasting pan. Place the stuffed veal on a rack over the onions, and add 1 to 2 cups of water (do not allow water to touch meat). Pour the remaining marinade over the meat and cover with heavy-duty foil. Bake for 3 hours. Remove the foil and bake about 1½ to 2 hours longer, basting every 30 minutes, until tender and brown. Slice, and serve with veal gravy.

Serves 12

Veal Gravy

2 tablespoons fat
  skimmed from the veal
  drippings
2 tablespoons potato
  starch
3 cups broth from veal
1 cup water
Salt and pepper to taste

In a 2-quart saucepan, mix the fat and the potato starch over medium-high heat with a wire whisk. Combine veal broth and water, and pour slowly into the pan, stirring continuously with a wire whisk until mixture begins to thicken. Season with salt and pepper.

Veal Stew

3 tablespoons chicken fat
¾ cup oil
3 cups cooked veal,
  cubed
3 stalks celery, chopped
1 medium onion,
  chopped
2 cloves garlic, chopped
4 to 6 fresh mushrooms,
  chopped
1 tablespoon fresh
  rosemary, chopped (or
  1 tsp. dried)
1½ cups chicken broth
1 cup tomato sauce (see
  conversion table)
3 tablespoons ketchup
2 tablespoons pareve
  margarine
1½ tablespoons potato
  starch
Pinch of salt
¼ teaspoon white pepper

This is a wonderful way to use your leftover veal roast.

1. Heat chicken fat and oil in a skillet over medium-high heat. Add veal and saute for a minute or two. Add chopped vegetables and rosemary; cook 5 to 10 minutes, stirring now and then. Remove from heat.

2. Combine chicken broth, tomato sauce, and ketchup. Heat margarine in a 2-quart saucepan; blend in potato starch, salt, and pepper with a wire whisk. Slowly add chicken broth mixture, stirring constantly. Add veal and vegetables. Stir well. Cover and cook over low heat for 30 minutes.

Serves 6 to 8

Roast Pickled Tongue

See Seder Menu #2 for recipe.

Veal Medallions Mirepoix

2 tablespoons oil
2 large carrots, peeled and diced
2 parsnips, peeled and diced
1 medium onion, chopped
¼ teaspoon thyme
Salt and pepper to taste
1 tablespoon pareve margarine
4 medallions of veal (eye of veal rib chop), 1-inch thick
1 tablespoon semi-sweet Passover wine
¼ teaspoon potato starch
½ teaspoon brandy

1. Heat oil in a large saute pan. Add carrots, parsnips, and onion and cook uncovered over medium heat until just tender and lightly colored, about 10 to 15 minutes. Cover for the last 5 minutes of cooking. Season with thyme, salt, and pepper, and set aside.

2. Heat margarine in the same pan. Brown the veal medallions over high heat. Season with salt and pepper. Drain off any excess margarine. Spread the sauteed vegetables over the veal, and cover the pan. (The dish may be prepared up to this point, refrigerated, and finished later.)

3. Cook slowly for 15 minutes. Remove the veal and vegetables to a serving platter and keep warm. Mix the wine and potato starch together with a fork. Add to juices in pan and let mixture come to a boil. Add the brandy and spoon over the veal. Delicious!!!

Serves 2

Turkey Schnitzel

8 turkey scallops
2 eggs
Pinch of salt
½ cup soup nut crumbs
¼ cup matzah meal
1 stick (½ cup) pareve margarine
½ cup oil
3 tablespoons lemon juice
½ cup chopped parlsey
Lemon wedges

1. Remove all fat from turkey scallops. Beat eggs and salt in a medium-sized bowl. Combine crumbs and matzah meal in a 9-inch pie plate.

2. Dip each turkey scallop in the egg mixture, making sure it is well covered, then dip in crumbs on both sides to coat thoroughly. Refrigerate for at least 30 minutes.

3. Heat margarine and oil in a large skillet. Saute scallops one at a time, 2 or 3 minutes on each side. Drain the grease from each scallop on paper towels, then place on serving platter.

4. Cook lemon juice and parsley in skillet for 1 minute on high heat. Pour over the scallops. Sprinkle with fresh chopped parsley and serve with lemon wedges.

Serves 6 to 8

Chicken Breasts with Mushroom Stuffing

5 whole chicken breasts,
skinned and boned
2 green onions, cut into
2-inch pieces
1 pound fresh
mushrooms
3 tablespoons pareve
margarine
¼ cup matzah farfel
Pinch of cumin
Pinch of turmeric
½ teaspoon salt
1 small piece of ginger
1½ cups chicken broth
1 teaspoon beef broth
mix
½ cup apricot preserves

Processor

1. Cut chicken breasts in half and pound them with the edge of a plate to flatten. Soak and drain the farfel. Preheat oven to 325°.

2. Insert metal blade. With the machine running, drop green onions through the feed tube, and process until minced. Add half the mushrooms and pulse 2 or 3 times. Add remaining mushrooms and pulse again. Scrape the sides of the bowl as necessary. Set aside.

3. Process farfel, cumin, turmeric, salt, and ginger with 3 pulses until fine.

4. Heat the margarine in a skillet. Saute the mushrooms and green onions. Stir in the farfel mixture. Spread 1 tablespoon on each piece of chicken. Roll from wide end to narrow end. Place in an open 9 x 13 baking dish.

5. Combine the chicken broth, beef broth mix, and apricot preserves and pour over the chicken. Bake for 1 hour, basting occasionally.

Conventional

Follow processor instructions, chopping vegetables with a knife. Farfel and seasonings may be chopped in a chopping bowl, or left unchopped for a different texture.

Serves 8 to 10

Note: At other times of the year you may make this with pineapple preserves.

Baked Breast of Chicken

See Seder Menu #1 for recipe.

Matzah Dressing

6 matzahs
2 tablespoons oil
¼ teaspoon chicken fat
1 large onion, chopped
3 stalks celery, chopped
2 large eggs, beaten
1 teaspoon salt
¼ teaspoon white pepper

You may also use this dressing to stuff a small chicken.

1. Preheat oven to 350° F. Grease a 1-quart casserole. Break up matzah and soak in 1 cup warm water until soft. Squeeze out water.

2. Heat oil and chicken fat in medium skillet over medium-high heat. Saute onion and celery until soft, add matzah and cook 5 minutes longer. Add beaten eggs, salt, and pepper.

3. Turn into the casserole and bake covered for 30 minutes. Uncover, turn oven to 400°, and bake until top is brown.

Serves 4 to 6

Desserts

Fillings, Frostings & Sauces

Vanilla Sugar

1 cup granulated sugar
1 vanilla bean

At Passover we're limited in the basic ingredients available for making fillings and frostings. Here are some easy substitutions you can make. It is also helpful to make several types of sugar syrup for flavoring cakes, cookies, and desserts.

Place the sugar in a 2-cup container with a tight-fitting lid. Cut the vanilla bean crosswise into several pieces and place over the sugar. Cover the container, and let stand for 24 hours before using. (For a better texture for baking, use your processor fitted with the metal blade, and process the sugar for 30 seconds.)

2 teaspoons of vanilla sugar equals 1 teaspoon of vanilla extract.

Confectioners' Sugar

1 cup less ½ tablespoon
  granulated sugar
½ tablespoon potato
  starch

Use food processor with metal blade, and process sugar for 30 seconds until very fine. Or you can pulverize it with an electric mixer. Sift sugar with potato starch, and store in an airtight container.

Flavored Confectioners' Sugar

Combine 1 cup confectioners' sugar with 1 teaspoon cinnamon, grated orange peel, or grated lemon peel.

Confectioners' Glaze

1 cup confectioners' sugar (see conversion table)
1 teaspoon lemon or orange juice
1 teaspoon grated lemon or orange peel

This is nice for glazing sponge cakes.

Combine sugar, juice, and grated peel. Gradually add 2 to 3 tablespoons hot water, stirring well after each addition, until the mixture coats the back of a spoon.

Apricot Glaze or Filling

Put apricot jam through a sieve or food mill, then heat over medium heat until boiling. Use to glaze cakes, fruit tarts, or pies. It is also wonderful for many poultry recipes. Keeps in the refrigerator for several weeks.

Lemon Filling

See Seder Menu #2 for recipe.

Whipped Cream Filling #1

1 cup whipping cream, chilled
1 tablespoon sugar
1 teaspoon vanilla (see conversion table)

Beat the cream with an electric mixer. When it begins to thicken, slowly add the sugar. Continue beating until it is thick enough to stand alone.

Fills a 9-inch 3-layer cake

Variation: Substitute coffee, cocoa, or brandy for the vanilla.

Whipped Cream Filling #2

1 cup whipping cream,
   chilled
½ cup jam (any flavor)
½ teaspoon lemon juice

Beat the cream with an electric mixer. Combine jam and lemon juice. When cream is thick enough to stand alone, fold in jam mixture.

Fills a 9-inch 3-layer cake

Meringue

See Seder Menu #2 for recipe.

Dried Fruit Filling

1 tablespoon potato
   starch
½ cup white raisins
¼ cup dates
¼ cup sugar
½ teaspoon lemon juice
Pinch of salt
¾ cup water
¼ cup chopped nuts

Processor

1. Mix potato starch with 1 tablespoon cold water until smooth. Set aside.

2. Insert metal blade. Place raisins, dates, sugar, lemon juice, and salt in work bowl. Pulse 3 or 4 times until chopped coarsely. Add water and process for 5 seconds.

3. Place in a 4-cup saucepan and cook on medium-high heat for 5 minutes. Stir in dissolved potato starch and cook 5 minutes longer. Remove from heat, mix in chopped nuts, and let cool.

Conventional

In step 2, chop raisins and dates with a sharp knife, and mix with remaining ingredients. Or place all ingredients in blender to chop and combine.

Fills a 2-layer cake

Orange Syrup

1 seedless orange, sliced
  very thin
1½ cups sugar
1 teaspoon lemon juice

Use for flavoring drinks and cakes, and for keeping moisture in cake layers. Keeps for more than a month in the refrigerator.

Place all ingredients in a medium saucepan with 3 cups of water. Bring to a boil, reduce heat to medium, and cook uncovered about 30 minutes, until a thick syrup is formed. Remove from heat, let cool, and pour into a jar. Makes about 2 cups.

Brandy Sauce

½ cup sugar
1 tablespoon potato
  starch
1 tablespoon grated
  lemon peel
4 tablespoons brandy,
  sherry, or wine

This is very good served warm over vanilla pudding.

Microwave

1. In a 4-cup microwave-safe measure, combine sugar and potato starch. Mix well with a fork. Add ½ cup water slowly and beat with a wire whisk until smooth. Cook on high setting for 2 minutes. Beat well with wire whisk and cook for 1 minute more or until thickened.

2. Add lemon peel and brandy; beat well.

Conventional

In step 1, mix ingredients in a saucepan. Cook over medium heat and stir continuously until thickened.

Makes 1 cup

Fudge Sauce

¾ cup sugar
3 tablespoons cocoa
Pinch of salt
⅔ cup evaporated milk
2 tablespoons butter or
   margarine
1 teaspoon vanilla (see
   conversion table)

In a 2-cup saucepan, combine sugar, cocoa, and salt. Blend in 2 tablespoons water, stirring until cocoa dissolves. Add milk and bring to a boil. Cook 3 to 4 minutes until sauce thickens, stirring frequently. Remove from heat. Stir in butter and vanilla.

Makes 1 cup

Chocolate Frosting

4 ounces semi-sweet
   chocolate
2 ounces unsalted butter
   or margarine
½ cup confectioners'
   sugar (see conversion
   table)
2 tablespoons brandy

Melt chocolate and butter in a 2-cup saucepan over medium heat. Remove from heat and add sugar, brandy, and 2 tablespoons hot water. Beat together until shiny and thick. Use immediately, or refrigerate and reheat.

Frosts a 10-inch torte

Cakes & Tortes

Chocolate Mousse Torte from Israel

6 eggs, separated
1½ cups sugar (divided)
2 sticks (½ pound) unsalted butter or margarine, softened
8 ounces semi-sweet chocolate, melted and cooled
½ cup chopped almonds
¼ cup brandy or orange juice
1 tablespoon matzah cake meal

Meringue

3 egg whites
¼ cup plus 1 tablespoon sugar
1 tablespoon potato starch
¼ cup water

If anyone had told me that my first trip to Israel in 1969 would send me home with a recipe that made me "famous," they didn't know the purpose of my trip. I was part of a United Jewish Appeal Women's Study Mission, and thinking about cooking was not on this agenda!

I had one free evening, however, and I took the opportunity to visit my adopted family, the Jerimiahus. Dena prepared an outstanding meal and the piece de resistance was her chocolate torte. Light as a feather, rich and moist, it melted in my mouth.

"There is no flour in it but there is one tablespoon of bread crumbs," said Dena.

"I must have the recipe," I said.

When Passover arrived, I was looking for something different to serve for dessert. Then I remembered Dena saying "no flour." I substituted matzah cake meal for the bread crumbs, and since then Dena's torte has graced many Passover tables. That first trip to Israel really turned out to be a "piece of cake!"

1. Preheat oven to 350° F. Grease a 9-inch springform pan and place a well-greased piece of wax paper on the bottom.

2. Beat egg whites until frothy. Slowly add ½ cup sugar, 2 tablespoons at a time, until whites hold a good peak but are not dry. Set aside.

3. Beat egg yolks in small mixer bowl until very thick and lemony in color, about 10 to 15 minutes. Add butter, 1 cup sugar, and melted chocolate. Beat 2 minutes.

4. Fold chopped nuts, flavoring, and cake meal into the remaining mixture. Remove 1 cup, and pour remainder into prepared

pan. Bake for 45 minutes or until cake begins to pull away from sides. (Refrigerate the reserved mixture.)

5. Remove from oven and cool for 15 minutes on a rack. Remove sides of pan. Let torte cool completely before inverting onto serving platter. Remove wax paper and spread reserved cup of chocolate mixture evenly over the top. Refrigerate, covered, 6 to 8 hours or overnight.

6. Preheat oven to 350° F.

7. Make the meringue. Combine 1 teaspoon potato starch with 1 tablespoon sugar and ¼ cup water in a small saucepan. Bring to a boil to thicken. Let cool.

8. Beat egg whites in small bowl of mixer. When whites form soft peaks, add ¼ cup sugar, 1 teaspoon at a time. Add boiled sugar mixture and continue beating until it holds stiff peaks. Spread over top and sides of torte. Place in oven for 10 minutes to brown. Turn off oven and leave torte in oven for 5 minutes. Refrigerate until serving time.

Serves 10 to 12

Note: For a dairy meal, you can use a whipped cream topping. Beat 1 pint whipping cream and 2 tablespoons sugar until stiff. Fold in 1 teaspoon vanilla (see conversion table) or raspberry syrup.

Chocolate "Genoise"

Filling

1 stick (½ cup) butter
8 ounces bittersweet
  chocolate
2 tablespoons brandy
6 large eggs, separated
1 cup sugar (divided)
½ cup whipping cream,
  chilled

Cake

1 stick (½ cup) butter
¼ cup matzah meal
¼ cup potato starch
¼ cup pecans
6 large eggs, separated
1¼ cup sugar
4 tablespoons cocoa
¼ cup brandy

Icing

1 cup whipping cream,
  chilled
1 teaspoon orange juice
2 tablespoons extra fine
  sugar

Chocolate curls or
chopped nuts for garnish

This cake takes a little time, but it's worth it—marvelous flavor and outstanding consistency.

Processor

1. Soften butter (may place in microwave for 45 seconds on low setting). Cut into 8 slices and set aside. Melt chocolate (may place in a 2-cup microwave-safe container and microwave for 2 minutes on high setting); stir in brandy, and let cool.

2. With electric mixer, beat egg whites on high speed. Add ¼ cup sugar, a little at a time, until whites hold stiff peaks but are not too dry. Set aside.

3. Insert metal blade. Process egg yolks with ¾ cup sugar for 2 minutes. Add butter and process 1 minute. Add melted chocolate and process 15 seconds. Fold into beaten egg whites.

4. With electric mixer, whip the cream until stiff, and fold into chocolate mixture. Refrigerate 1 or 2 hours.

1. Preheat oven to 350° F. Cut wax paper to fit the bottom of a 10-inch springform pan; grease well.

2. Soften butter (may place in microwave on low setting for 45 seconds). Cut into 8 pieces.

3. Insert metal blade. Place matzah cake meal, potato starch, and nuts in work bowl and process for 10 seconds. Set aside.

4. With electric mixer, beat egg whites until soft peaks begin to form. Add ¼ cup sugar, a little at a time, until egg whites hold stiff peaks.

5. Process egg yolks with ¾ cup sugar for 2 minutes. Add cocoa, brandy, and ¼ cup sugar and process 15 seconds. Add reserved dry ingredients and pulse only until they disappear. Fold into egg whites. Pour

into pan and bake 40 to 50 minutes. Remove from oven and cool completely on a rack.

6. Remove wax paper and split cake in half. Spread one layer with chocolate filling. Top with the other layer and ice with the whipped cream that has been beaten with orange juice and extra fine sugar until stiff. Decorate with chocolate curls or chopped nuts. Refrigerator for several hours before serving.

Serves 12 to 16

Chocolate Nut Torte

6 eggs, separated
1½ cups sugar
1 cup walnuts
½ cup semi-sweet
   chocolate pieces
2 apples, peeled and
   cored
1 cup matzah cake meal

Processor

1. Preheat oven to 350° F. Grease a 9-inch springform pan.

2. Insert metal blade. Place egg yolks and sugar in work bowl and process for 60 seconds. Add nuts and chocolate pieces, and process 5 seconds. Add apples, cut into quarters, and pulse 3 or 4 times. Add cake meal and process 5 seconds.

3. Beat egg whites until stiff with an electric mixer. Fold into chocolate batter. Pour into prepared pan and bake 50 to 60 minutes. Let cool 15 minutes before removing sides of pan.

Conventional

In step 2, beat together egg yolks and sugar with electric mixer. Chop together nuts and apples and combine with egg yolks. Add cake meal and fold in chocolate pieces. Proceed to step 3.

Serves 10 to 12

Chocolate Cake #1

9 eggs
1½ cups sugar (divided)
½ cup oil
⅓ cup water
Juice and grated peel of 1
    orange
½ cup matzah cake meal
½ cup potato starch
¼ cup cocoa
½ teaspoon salt

1. Preheat oven to 350° F. Grease a 10-inch tube pan.

2. Beat the egg yolks with electric mixer until stiff. Add 1 cup sugar and beat until pale yellow. Mix in oil, water, orange juice, and peel. Beat well.

3. Sift together cake meal, potato starch, and cocoa. Add to the batter and beat for 10 minutes.

4. In a separate bowl, beat egg whites with salt. Add remaining ½ cup sugar a little at a time until whites are stiff but not dry. Fold into egg yolk mixture. Pour into prepared pan and bake 50 to 60 minutes.

5. If desired, split cake in half when cool, fill with jam, and ice.

Serves 12 to 16

Chocolate Cake #2

9 eggs, separated
1½ cup sugar
½ cup matzah meal
½ cup potato starch
½ teaspoon salt
2 tablespoons cocoa
2 ounces melted
  bittersweet chocolate
⅓ cup milk
Juice and grated peel of 1
  orange

1. Preheat oven to 350° F. Grease a 10-inch springform pan.

2. With electric mixer, beat egg yolks with 1 cup of sugar until thick.

3. Sift together matzah meal, potato starch, salt, and cocoa. Mix into egg yolks. Add melted chocolate, milk, orange juice, and peel. Beat for 10 minutes. Set aside.

4. In a separate bowl, beat egg whites with remaining ½ cup of sugar, adding the sugar a little at a time until egg whites become stiff but not dry. Fold into the egg yolk mixture.

5. Pour into prepared pan and bake 50 to 60 minutes. Remove from oven and let cool 15 minutes on a rack. Remove sides of pan and let cool completely. Ice cake if desired.

Serves 12 to 16

Macaroon Torte

4 dozen stale macaroons
8 egg yolks
1½ cup brown sugar
1 quart whipping cream, chilled
1 tablespoon brandy
1 cup raspberry syrup

This is a wonderful dessert for a large party. It looks good, may be made ahead of time, and tastes delicious! It will keep in the freezer up to one month.

1. To make crumbs with food processor, use metal blade. Crumble macaroons in work bowl, and process for about 15 seconds.

2. With electric mixer, beat the egg yolks and sugar until very thick, about 10 minutes. Set aside.

3. Beat whipping cream in a large bowl until stiff. Fold in 1 cup of egg yolks with a wire whisk. Fold in remaining egg yolks, macaroons, and brandy with a rubber spatula.

4. Turn into a 10-inch springform pan, and freeze. One hour before serving, unmold and slice. Pour some raspberry syrup over each serving.

Serves 20

Passover Sponge Cake

See Seder Menu #1 for recipe.

Hazelnut Torte

8 large eggs, separated
1 cup sugar
1 teaspoon vanilla (see
 conversion table)
1 cup finely ground
 hazelnuts
1 whole egg
1 teaspoon lemon juice
Chocolate Glaze (recipe
 follows)

1. Preheat oven to 350° F. Grease a 9-inch springform pan.

2. Beat egg whites with electric mixer until stiff but not dry. Set aside.

3. Beat egg yolks and sugar with electric mixer until thick and lemony in color, about 5 minutes. Add remaining ingredients and continue beating until well mixed.

4. Carefully fold egg whites into the egg yolk batter. Pour into prepared pan and bake for 45 minutes or until browned.

5. Turn off oven and let cool in oven, about 30 to 45 minutes. The cake will rise at first and then fall a little in the center, but it will taste delicious.

6. Place cake on rack. Pour Chocolate Glaze over cake lightly, smoothing the sides. Refrigerate for 30 minutes before placing on serving platter.

Serves 10 to 12

Chocolate Glaze

2 ounces semi-sweet
 chocolate, broken into
 small pieces.
1 tablespoon brandy
3 tablespoons butter or
 margarine

Melt the chocolate with the brandy. (You may place in a 1-quart microwave-safe container and microwave on high for about 1 minute, or melt over hot water in a double boiler). Beat in butter, 1 tablespoon at a time, until the glaze has cooled and is of pouring consistency, about 5 minutes.

Hazelnut Roll

Cake

6 eggs, separated
¾ cup sugar
1½ cups chopped
  hazelnuts
¼ teaspoon baking soda
½ teaspoon cream of
  tartar

Filling

3 cups whipping cream,
  chilled
¼ cup sugar
2 teaspoons coffee or
  brandy

1. Preheat oven to 350° F. Grease a 10 x 14 jelly-roll pan. Line the pan with wax paper and grease the paper.

2. Beat egg whites with electric mixer until soft peaks begin to form. Add ½ cup sugar, a little at a time, until stiff peaks are formed. Set aside.

3. Beat egg yolks until thick. Add the remaining sugar and continue beating until pale yellow. Combine chopped hazelnuts, baking soda, and cream of tartar, and mix into egg yolks. Fold into the stiffly beaten egg whites. Spread evenly in the pan. Bake for 20 minutes.

4. Turn out onto a clean linen tea towel to cool. (See illustration for Lemon Cake Roll.) Remove wax paper and immediately roll the cake and towel loosely the long way, and let cool for about 20 minutes.

5. For the filling, beat the whipping cream and sugar until stiff. Fold in coffee. Unroll cake, and spread evenly with the filling. Roll from the long side forward. Place seam side down on a serving platter. Serve plain or with Chocolate Glaze.

Serves 8 to 10

Passover Lemon Cake Roll

See Seder Menu #2 for recipe.

Cheesecake

Crust

2 cups pecans
3 tablespoons sugar
1 teaspoon cinnamon
¼ teaspoon ginger
6 tablespoons butter or
  margarine

Filling

8 ounces farmers cheese
8 ounces cream cheese
1 cup dry cottage cheese
3 eggs
3 tablespoons sugar
½ teaspoon lemon juice
1 teaspoon lemon peel

Processor

1. Preheat oven to 350° F.

2. Make the crust: Using the metal blade, chop pecans very fine. Add remaining ingredients to work bowl and process 25 seconds. Press mixture into the bottom and up the sides of a 9-inch springform pan. Set aside.

3. Make the filling: Cut farmers cheese and cream cheese into 1-inch cubes and process with all remaining ingredients until smooth (about 40 to 50 seconds), scraping the bowl as necessary.

4. Pour into crust and bake 45 to 50 minutes. Cool on a rack, remove sides of pan, and refrigerate for several hours, preferably overnight.

Conventional

In step 2, chop nuts by hand and blend in remaining ingredients. In step 3, use electric mixer to beat cheeses with sugar. Add remaining ingredients and beat until smooth.

Serves 12 to 14

Miniature Cheesecakes

3 packages (8 oz. each)
  cream cheese
1 cup sugar
1½ teaspoons lemon
  juice
5 eggs

Topping

1½ cups sour cream
¼ cup plus 2 tablespoons
  sugar
½ teaspoon vanilla (see
  conversion table)

Processor

1. Preheat oven to 300° F. Place cupcake liners in miniature cupcake pans.

2. Use metal blade to process cream cheese, sugar, and lemon juice until creamy (about 1 minute). Add eggs one at a time through the feed tube, blending thoroughly after each one. Scrape sides of bowl as necessary. Process for 15 seconds after last egg is added.

3. Fill cupcake cups ⅔ full. Bake for 35 minutes. Remove from oven and turn oven off.

4. Combine topping ingredients in work bowl and process 10 seconds. Spread 1 teaspoon on each cheesecake. Return to turned-off oven for 10 minutes. Refrigerate for several hours.

Makes 18

Pies & Tarts

Custard Pie

½ cup sugar
2 tablespoons potato
  starch
2 large eggs
1 cup sour cream
9-inch unbaked pie shell

Processor

1. Preheat oven to 300° F.

2. Insert metal blade. Place sugar and potato starch in work bowl and pulse once or twice. Add eggs and sour cream; process 30 seconds.

3. Pour into pie shell and bake 1 hour or until the custard is set. Cool before serving.

Conventional

In step 2, blend all ingredients with a wire whisk or rotary beater.

Serves 6 to 8

Variation: Add fresh fruit on the bottom of the pie shell, or add a tablespoon of juice or syrup to the custard.

Glazed Peach Pie

5 cups sliced fresh
  peaches (about 2½ lbs.)
¾ cup sugar
1 teaspoon lemon juice
½ tablespoon potato
  starch
¼ teaspoon salt
½ teaspoon nutmeg
9-inch unbaked pie shell
1 cup toasted sliced
  almonds
½ cup apricot preserves

This is an attractive and easy-to-make dessert.

1. Preheat oven to 425° F. Combine sliced peaches, sugar, and lemon juice. Sift together potato starch, salt, and nutmeg, and stir into peaches.

2. Arrange peaches in a circular pattern in the pie shell. Sprinkle evenly with the almonds.

3. Bake for 20 minutes, then cover with foil and bake 20 to 25 minutes longer. Remove pie from oven and remove foil. Melt apricot preserves in a small saucepan and brush over the top of the peaches. Cool.

Serves 8

Topping for Fruit Pies

1 cup matzah cake meal
1 cup brown sugar
1 stick (½ cup soft butter
or margarine
½ cup chopped pecans

With fingertips, crumble cake meal, sugar, and butter into a coarse meal. Stir in the chopped pecans. Sprinkle evenly over any fruit pie and bake in a preheated 450° oven for 45 minutes.

For an 8- or 9-inch pie

Miniature Pecan Tarts

Dough

1 cup butter or margarine
8 ounces cream cheese
2 cups sifted matzah cake
meal

Filling

2 cups brown sugar
3 eggs
1 tablespoon melted
butter or margarine
1 teaspoon vanilla (see
conversion table)
1 cup pecans, coarsely
chopped

Processor

1. Insert metal blade. Cut butter and cream cheese into 1-inch cubes and process for 6 seconds. Add cake meal and pulse 2 or 3 times, until it just disappears.

2. Divide dough among 48 ungreased miniature muffin tins, using thumb to push down into the bottom and up the sides of each cup. Refrigerate while making filling.

3. Preheat oven to 350° F.

4. Place all filling ingredients except pecans in work bowl, and process 30 seconds or until well mixed. Set aside. Chop pecans with 2 or 3 pulses.

5. Remove dough from refrigerator. Place ¼ teaspoon chopped pecans in each cup. Cover with 1 teaspoon filling. Bake for 15 to 20 minutes.

Conventional

In step 1, use electric mixer to beat cream cheese and butter together with cake meal. In step 4, use electric mixer to blend all ingredients except pecans. Chop pecans by hand.

Makes 4 dozen

Jam Tarts

Dough

¾ cup whole blanched almonds
½ cup matzah cake meal
¼ cup potato starch
⅓ cup sugar
1 stick (½ cup) frozen butter or margarine, cut into 8 pieces
1 large egg

Filling

1½ cups jam (apricot, strawberry, raspberry)
½ cup chopped nuts or macaroon crumbs

Processor

1. Insert metal blade. Chop almonds 10 seconds until coarsely chopped. Add remaining dough ingredients. Pulse 3 or 4 times, then process 5 seconds.

2. Divide the dough into 24 greased muffin cups. Press gently onto the bottom and sides. Refrigerate 30 minutes.

3. Preheat oven to 400° F.

4. Combine jam and nuts, and spoon evenly onto the dough. Bake 10 minutes or until tarts are golden in color. Cool 15 to 20 minutes before removing from pans. Serve plain or topped with whipped cream.

Conventional

In step 1, chop almonds and combine with matzah cake meal, potato starch, and sugar. Have butter at room temperature, and blend into the nut mixture. Add well-beaten egg and blend thoroughly. Proceed to step 2.

Makes 24

Passover Pie Crust #1

1 cup matzah meal
3 tablespoons plus 1
   teaspoon sugar
6 tablespoons butter or
   margarine, cut in 8
   pieces

Processor

1. Preheat oven to 375° F. Grease a 9-inch pie pan.
2. Insert metal blade. Place all ingredients in work bowl and process until well blended, about 25 to 30 seconds.
3. Press into the bottom and up the sides of pie pan. Bake 18 to 20 minutes. Cool completely before filling.

Conventional

In step 2, combine ingredients with a pastry blender or electric mixer.

Passover Pie Crust #2

1⅓ cups stale macaroons,
   crumbled
1 stick (½ cup) butter or
   margarine, cut in 8
   pieces
¼ cup sugar
¼ teaspoon cinnamon

Processor

1. Preheat oven to 375° F.
2. Insert metal blade. Place macaroons in work bowl and process until fine crumbs form, about 15 to 20 seconds; add remaining ingredients and process until well blended.
3. Press crust into the bottom and up the sides of an ungreased 9-inch pie pan. Bake for 7 minutes until golden brown. Cool completely before filling.

Conventional

In step 2, make cookie crumbs by hand or with a blender; combine ingredients with a pastry blender or electric mixer.

Note: When recipe calls for an unbaked pie shell, fill before baking.

Passover Pie Crust #3

1½ cups pecans
3 tablespoons sugar
3 tablespoons soft butter
  or margarine
⅓ cup matzah cake meal

Processor

1. Preheat oven to 400° F. Grease a 9-inch pie pan.
2. Insert metal blade. Place pecans in work bowl and process until fine, with 3 or 4 pulses. Add remaining ingredients and process until well blended, about 15 to 20 seconds.
3. Press into bottom and up the sides of pie pan. Bake 8 to 10 minutes or until light gold in color. Cool completely before filling.

Conventional

In step 2, chop nuts by hand or with a blender; combine ingredients with a pastry blender or electric mixer.

Note: When recipe calls for an unbaked pie shell, fill before baking.

Passover Pie Crust #4

1 cup toasted almonds
½ cup matzah meal
3 tablespoons sugar
1 egg
2 tablespoons soft butter

Processor

1. Preheat oven to 400° F. Grease a 9-inch pie pan.

2. Insert metal blade. Place almonds in work bowl and chop fine with 3 or 4 pulses. Add remaining ingredients and process until well blended, about 15 to 20 seconds.

3. Press into the bottom and up the sides of pie pan. Refrigerate for 1 hour before baking.

4. Bake for 8 to 10 minutes or until light gold in color. Cool completely before filling.

Conventional

In step 2, chop nuts by hand or with a blender; combine ingredients with a pastry blender or electric mixer.

Note: When recipe calls for an unbaked pie shell, fill before baking.

Cookies

Passover Cookie Dough

1 cup butter or margarine
1 cup sugar
3 eggs
2 cups less 2 tablespoons matzah cake meal
2 tablespoons potato starch
¼ teaspoon salt
Juice and peel of medium lemon

While I was attending a meeting during Passover at my friend Debbie Fox's house, I saw that the table was laden with a variety of cookies. Naturally, I had to get the recipes. When I found out they all came from one basic dough, I was delighted. Debbie asked me to share these with you.

Processor

Insert metal blade. Place butter and sugar into work bowl. Process until creamy (about 60 seconds). Add eggs, cake meal, potato starch, and salt. Pulse several times until well mixed. Add lemon juice and peel. Mix well. Use to make recipes that follow.

Conventional

Beat butter and sugar in bowl of electric mixer for about 10 minutes until creamy. Add eggs and beat 5 minutes more. Sift cake meal, potato starch, and salt. Add to batter. Mix in lemon juice and peel. Use to make recipes that follow.

Birds' Nests

1 recipe Passover Cookie Dough
Cinnamon-sugar mixture
Raspberry jam

Roll dough into balls, coat with cinnamon-sugar mixture, and place balls on greased cookie sheet. Press finger to indent centers, fill with jam, and bake at 350° F for 8 to 10 minutes. Makes about 2 dozen.

Toasted Cinnamon Sugar Slices

1 recipe Passover Cookie Dough
½ cup almonds
½ cup walnuts
Cinnamon-sugar mixture

Grind almonds and walnuts, and add to dough. Roll into 2-inch loaves. Bake at 350° for 20 to 25 minutes. Slice, sprinkle with cinnamon-sugar mixture, and return to oven. Toast on each side for 5 minutes. Makes about 3 dozen.

Jam Squares

1 recipe Passover Cookie
  Dough
1 jar (12 oz.) preserves
  (cherry, apricot,
  raspberry)
½ chopped nuts
½ cup raisins

Press half the dough into a greased 8-inch square pan. Cover evenly with preserves, nuts, and raisins. Roll remaining dough between 2 sheets of plastic wrap; remove plastic and place dough over the top. Bake at 350° for 30 minutes. Cut into squares. Makes 25.

Lemon Squares

1 recipe Passover Cookie
  Dough
4 eggs
2 cups sugar
2 tablespoons potato
  starch
Juice from 2 lemons
Confectioners' sugar (see
  conversion table)

Wet hands and press Cookie Dough into a 9-inch square pan. Bake at 350° for 10 minutes and remove from oven. Combine the eggs, sugar, potato starch, and lemon juice. Pour over baked crust and return to the oven for 30 minutes. Cool, top with confectioners' sugar, and cut into squares. Makes 25.

Forgotten Cookies

2 egg whites
¾ cup sugar
1 teaspoon vanilla (see
  conversion table)
¼ teaspoon salt
1 cup broken pecans
1 cup chocolate chips

These are so easy and so sweet, you'll love them!

1. Preheat oven to 350° F. Line 2 cookie sheets with foil.

2. With electric mixer, beat egg whites until peaks begin to form. Add sugar slowly (about 1 tablespoon at a time). Add vanilla and salt and beat until everything is very stiff and very shiny.

3. Fold in pecans and chocolate chips. Drop by teaspoons onto the prepared cookie sheets and place in preheated oven. Turn off the oven and "forget" the cookies until the next morning.

Makes about 3 dozen

Almond-Orange Peel Macaroons

Peel of 1 large navel
  orange
2 tablespoons potato
  starch
½ cup sugar
1 cup blanched almonds
1 teaspoon cinnamon
½ teaspoon nutmeg
2 egg whites

Processor

1. Preheat oven to 350° F. Cover a cookie sheet with greased aluminum foil.

2. Remove peel from orange with sharp knife or zester. Try not to include any white pith because it is bitter.

3. Beat egg whites until stiff and set aside.

4. Insert metal blade. Place the peel, potato starch, and sugar in work bowl, and process for 30 seconds. Add almonds and spices. Process until well blended and almonds look like bread crumbs (not too fine), about 3 minutes.

5. Remove mixture to a large bowl and fold in egg whites. Form into walnut-sized balls, handling lightly. Place balls on cookie sheet about 3 inches apart; they will spread out when baking.

6. Bake at 350° for 5 minutes. Turn oven to 400° and continue baking until cookies are lightly brown (about 10 to 12 minutes). Cool before removing from cookie sheet.

Conventional

In step 4, grate orange peel. Grind almonds in blender or nut grinder (not too fine; should look like bread crumbs).

Makes about 2 dozen

Mandelbrot

¼ cup chopped almonds
¼ cup chopped walnuts
4 eggs
1 cup sugar
1 cup oil
Juice and grated peel of 1 orange
Juice and grated peel of 1 lemon
1½ cups matzah cake meal
1 tablespoon potato starch
¼ teaspoon nutmeg
Cinnamon-sugar mixture for topping

Some women have "my son the doctor," but I have "my niece the doctor." Every year we count on Dr. Mindy Hastie to bring the mandelbrot for the family Seder. She got this recipe from her Aunt Fannie in Louisville. It wouldn't be Passover without Mindy's mandelbrot! What would we nosh on the rest of the week?

Processor

1. Insert metal blade. Chop nuts with 3 or 4 pulses and set aside.

2. Place eggs, sugar, oil, juices, and peels in work bowl, and process for 15 seconds. Add cake meal, potato starch, and nutmeg and process just until the mixture disappears. Add the chopped nuts and pulse 2 or 3 times.

3. Preheat the oven to 375° F.

4. Sprinkle a board lightly with cake meal. Place the dough on the board, and form into long rolls, about 3 inches wide and 1 inch thick. Place on cookie sheet and sprinkle all over with cinnamon-sugar mixture. Bake 30 to 45 minutes or until light brown in color.

5. Cut each loaf into ½-inch slices. Place each slice cut-side-up on the cookie sheet, sprinkle with cinnamon-sugar, and place in the oven to toast. Turn slices over and sprinkle with cinammon-sugar to toast the other side.

Conventional

Sift together the dry ingredients. Mix together eggs, oil, sugar, grated peel, and juice with electric mixer. Add sifted dry ingredients. Fold in nuts. Proceed to step 3.

Makes about 3 dozen

Lace Cookies

½ cup sugar
1½ teaspoons potato starch
2 tablespoons milk
¾ cup finely chopped almonds
1 stick (½ cup) unsalted butter

1. Combine sugar and potato starch in a 1-quart saucepan. Stir in the milk. Add remaining ingredients. Bring to a boil over medium heat, stirring constantly. Remove from heat and let cool. Refrigerate for 1 hour.

2. Preheat oven to 350° F. Line a cookie sheet with foil. Grease the foil and sprinkle with cake meal. Drop dough onto the sheet by the teaspoon, 3 inches apart to allow for spreading (these cookies really spread!). Bake 6 to 7 minutes. Let cool. Remove the foil from the cookie sheet and gently shake off the cookies.

Makes 15 to 18

Passover Fudge Squares

½ cup matzah cake meal
½ cup potato starch
½ teaspoon salt
4 tablespoons or more cocoa (unsweetened)
4 eggs
2 cups sugar
1 cup oil
2 cups pecans or walnuts, chopped

Conventional

1. Preheat oven to 325° F.

2. Mix dry ingredients together and reserve. Beat eggs and sugar until thick and fluffy. Add oil and mix well.

3. Add dry ingredients and blend well. Stir in chopped nuts and spread in an oiled 8- or 9-inch square pan. Bake for 35 minutes. Cool slightly and cut into squares.

Processor

Place dry ingredients in work bowl (metal blade) and pulse several times to mix; remove. Add eggs and sugar to work bowl and process 1 minute. Add oil and process several seconds to mix well. In step 2, add dry ingredients and pulse until combined. Add whole nuts and pulse to chop and mix in.

Makes 25

Mock Oatmeal Cookies

2 cups matzah meal
2 cups matzah farfel
1 cup sugar
½ cup brown sugar
½ cup walnuts
⅔ cup oil
4 large eggs
2 teaspoons cinnamon
½ teaspoon salt
½ cup raisins

These have a little different taste and consistency from the ones we are used to the rest of the year. They freeze wonderfully and keep well in tins. For a softer cookie, add another egg.

Processor

1. Preheat oven to 350° F. Grease a cookie sheet.

2. Insert metal blade. Place matzah meal, farfel, and sugars in work bowl and pulse 2 times. Remove to a large bowl.

3. Place walnuts in work bowl and pulse to chop. Remove from bowl. Add oil, eggs, cinnamon, and salt to work bowl, and process for 15 seconds. Pour over dry ingredients and mix well. Fold in raisins and walnuts.

4. Drop by teaspoonfuls on the cookie sheet, 2 inches apart. Bake 30 to 35 minutes.

Makes 3 to 4 dozen

Toffee Squares

1 cup butter or margarine
1 large egg
1 cup sugar
1 teaspoon vanilla (see
  conversion table)
¼ teaspoon salt
  (optional)
1 cup matzah cake meal
8 ounces semi-sweet
  chocolate
1 cup pecans

Processor

1. Preheat oven to 350° F. Lightly grease a 10 x 15 jelly roll pan.

2. Insert metal blade. Place butter, egg, sugar, vanilla, and salt in work bowl. Process until light and fluffy, scraping down sides at least once after about 10 seconds.

3. Add half the cake meal to the bowl and process until it disappears. Add the other half and process for 30 seconds. Dough should be very stiff. You may need to add 1 or 2 more tablespoons of cake meal to get the dough to the right consistency.

4. Spread the dough in the pan, making sure it covers all the corners. Bake for 20 minutes.

5. Melt chocolate and spread over baked dough.

6. Chop pecans with 3 or 4 pulses. Sprinkle evenly over dough. Let cool 15 minutes. Cut into squares before completely cooled.

Conventional

In steps 2 and 3, use an electric mixer. In step 6, chop nuts by hand.

Makes about 36

Apple Squares

2 cups less 2 tablespoons matzah cake meal
2 tablespoons potato starch
¼ teaspoon salt
1 cup butter or margarine
1½ cups sugar (divided)
4 eggs
Juice and grated peel of 1 lemon
3 large cooking apples, peeled and cored
½ cup white raisins
1 teaspoon cinnamon
¼ teaspoon ground nutmeg

Processor

1. Preheat oven to 375° F. Grease a 9-inch square cake pan.

2. Insert metal blade. Place cake meal, potato starch, and salt in work bowl and process 35 seconds. Set aside.

3. Cut butter into 1-inch chunks. Place in work bowl with sugar and process 30 seconds. Scrape the bowl and process 30 seconds longer. Add eggs through the feed tube one at a time with machine running. Add juice and peel. Process 3 or 4 seconds. Add the dry ingredients and pulse 2 or 3 times just until they disappear.

4. With wet hands, press half the dough into the pan. Slice the apples evenly on top. Sprinkle with raisins. Combine remaining ½ cup of sugar with cinnamon and nutmeg, and sprinkle evenly over raisins and apples.

5. Crumble remaining dough over fruit. Bake 45 to 50 minutes. Cool 30 minutes and cut into 12 squares.

Conventional

In step 2, sift cake meal, potato starch, and salt. In step 3, cream the butter and 1 cup of sugar in large bowl of electric mixer; add eggs, lemon rind, and juice. Beat for 1 minute. Add sifted dry ingredients. Mix well. Proceed to step 4.

Makes 12

Apricot Bars

Dough

1 stick (½ cup) butter or
  margarine, cut into 8
  pieces
1 cup sifted matzah cake
  meal
¼ cup sugar

Filling

⅔ cup dried apricots
1 cup brown sugar
¼ cup matzah cake meal
¼ teaspoon salt
2 large eggs
½ teaspoon vanilla (see
  conversion table)
½ cup chopped pecans

Processor

1. Preheat oven to 350° F.

2. Insert metal blade. Place all dough ingredients into work bowl, and pulse 2 or 3 times until crumbly. Pat into the bottom of a 8-inch square pan, and bake for 15 minutes until slightly brown.

3. Chop apricots with 2 or 3 pulses. Place in a 1-quart saucepan and add only enough water to cover. Bring to boil over medium-high heat and boil 10 minutes. Let cool in liquid.

4. Place brown sugar, matzah cake meal, salt, eggs, and vanilla in work bowl, and process 10 seconds. Add cooked apricots, cooking liquid, and nuts. Pulse 1 or 2 times, until they just disappear. Pour onto baked crust. Return to oven and bake 30 minutes. Cut into bars when cool.

Conventional

In step 2, use an electric mixer. In step 3, cut up apricots with a sharp knife. In step 4, use electric mixer.

Makes 24

Apricot Nut Bars

1 cup dried apricots
¾ cup matzah meal
1 cup finely chopped
   pecans or walnuts
⅓ cup sugar
½ cup butter or
   margarine
½ cup soup nuts
½ cup apricot preserves
¼ cup orange juice
2 teaspoons grated
   orange peel

Processor

1. Preheat oven to 350° F. Grease and flour a 9-inch square pan.

2. Cook dried apricots in water to just cover. Let come to boil, then simmer for 10 minutes. Cool and drain.

3. Place matzah meal, nuts, and sugar in work bowl and process with metal blade until nuts are chopped fine (about 30 seconds). Add butter; process with 3 or 4 pulses until mixture is crumbly and moist. Reserve ¼ cup of this mixture for topping, and firmly pat remainder into the bottom of the pan, making a solid dough base.

4. Place cooked apricots, soup nuts, preserves, orange juice, and peel in work bowl. Pulse one or two times, then process until well mixed, about 30 seconds. Spread carefully over dough in pan. Sprinkle with reserved topping. Bake for 30 minutes. Cool, and cut into squares.

Makes 25

Apricot-Nut Balls

1 pound dried apricots
1 seedless orange, peeled
   and sliced
½ cup pecans or walnuts
1 teaspoon brandy
¼ teaspoon ginger
1 cup toasted coconut or
   1 cup finely ground
   nuts

Keep these on hand as snacks. They are easy to make and disappear very quickly.

Processor

1. Insert metal blade and process apricots, orange, nuts, brandy, and ginger for 1 minute or until fruit and nuts are finely ground. Scrape sides of bowl as necessary.

2. Form into small balls. Place on cake rack to dry for 30 minutes. Roll in coconut or nuts. Store in tightly covered container.

Conventional

In step 1, use a food grinder.

Makes 4 to 5 dozen

Dried Fruit Delights

1 cup pitted dates
1 cup pitted prunes
1 cup raisins
1 cup dried figs
2 tablespoons brandy
1 tablespoon ground
  ginger
1 cup walnuts
1 cup finely ground nuts

Processor

1. Soak the dried fruits in boiling water to cover, for approximately 10 minutes. Drain, and pat dry.

2. Insert metal blade. Place dates, prunes, raisins, figs, brandy, and ginger in the work bowl. Pulse several times. Add walnuts, and process until fruits and nuts are chopped very fine. Scrape sides of bowl as necessary.

3. Form into balls the size of a large olive. Place on wire rack to dry slightly. Roll in ground nuts and store in a tightly covered container.

Conventional

In step 2, use a food grinder.

Makes 5 to 6 dozen

Fruit Desserts

Baked Apple Slices

6 Golden Delicious
  apples, peeled, cored,
  and sliced
¼ cup sugar
Juice and grated peel of 1
  lemon
¼ cup melted butter or
  margarine
2 tablespoons solid butter
  or margarine

This is one of my family's favorite dishes when we're having any fowl.

1. As you cut the apples, put the slices in cold water. When ready to bake, remove with slotted spoon and dry with paper towels. Combine the sugar, lemon juice and peel, and melted margarine.

2. Preheat oven to 325°. Arrange apple slices in rows in a shallow baking dish. Spoon half the sugar-lemon mixture over the apples. Bake for 20 minutes and remove from oven.

3. Turn oven to broil. Spoon remaining sugar-lemon mixture over the apples and dot with butter. Broil 4 inches from the heat for 1 to 2 minutes or until edges begin to brown.

Serves 6

Brandied Fresh Grapes

3 pounds green seedless
  grapes
½ cup honey
3 tablespoons lemon juice
8 tablespoons brandy
Sour cream
Brown sugar

This is an easy dessert for a party.

Place grapes in a large serving bowl. Combine honey, lemon juice, and brandy and pour over grapes. Stir well. Let marinate for 3 to 5 hours. To serve, top with sour cream and brown sugar.

Serves 12 to 16

Apple-Barb

1 pound rhubarb, cut
  into 1-inch pieces
1 pound tart apples
  (McIntosh or Granny
  Smith), peeled, cored,
  and sliced
½ cup sugar
½ teaspoon ground
  ginger
¼ teaspoon ground
  cardamon

This is a delicious accompaniment for any meat or fowl dish, or a lovely dessert.

Microwave

Place rhubarb and apples in a 2-quart microwave-safe bowl; combine remaining ingredients and mix in. Cover with vented plastic wrap and microwave on high setting for 10 minutes. Let cool.

Conventional

Place rhubarb and apples in 2-quart saucepan; add remaining ingredients. Cover and bring slowly to a boil. Turn down and simmer for 10 minutes. Transfer to serving bowl and let cool.

Serves 6 to 8

Poached Pears

6 ripe pears
6 whole cloves
1 cup sugar
½ cup white wine (I
  prefer Chablis)
¼ cup water

Microwave

1. Peel pears, leaving the stems in place. Stick 1 clove into each pear.

2. Combine the remaining ingredients in a 1 ½-quart casserole. Add pears, laying them on their sides. Cover with vented plastic wrap. Cook on high setting for 6 to 8 minutes. Baste pears with syrup, turn on other side, and continue cooking on high for 6 to 8 minutes more or until pears are tender. Test for doneness with toothpick or fork.

3. Serve warm with whipping cream or chocolate sauce. You may also dip them in melted chocolate and place in freezer for 10 minutes before serving.

Serves 6

Hot Brandied Fruit

1 pound dried apricots
3 cans (16 oz. each) peach halves
1 navel orange, peeled and sliced
½ pound pitted prunes
1 cup brown sugar
¼ cup brandy

1. Drain the juice from the canned peaches into a 1-quart measuring cup. Place the peaches on paper towels, cut side down, to drain.

2. Cook dried apricots in 1 cup water about 10 to 15 minutes, until soft. Drain; add liquid to peach juice to make 3 cups.

3. Place orange slices in a medium saucepan. Add the apricot-peach juice and bring to a boil. Turn to simmer and cook for 30 minutes.

4. Preheat oven to 400° F. Place peaches, cut side up, in a 9 x 11½ baking dish, and place a pitted prune and a cooked apricot in each cavity. Pour cooked oranges evenly over all. Dot with brown sugar. Bake for 30 minutes.

5. To serve, pour brandy over the fruit and return to oven for 10 minutes (or microwave on high setting for 3 minutes). Serve warm.

Serves 10

Hot Spiced Fruits

1 cup sugar
1 cup white wine
½ cup honey
12 whole cloves
1 teaspoon ground
  cinnamon, nutmeg,
  ginger, and coriander,
  or to taste
1 stick (½ cup) butter or
  margarine
1 can (16 oz.) apricots
  halves, drained
1 can (16 oz.) sliced
  peaches, drained
1 can (16 oz.) pear halves,
  drained
1 can (16 oz.) pineapple
  chunks, drained
½ pound seedless green
  grapes
½ pound seedless red
  grapes
2 bananas, sliced

1. Combine sugar, wine, honey, spices, and butter in a 6-quart pot. Cook over low heat until butter melts. Add canned fruit and bring to a boil. Turn to simmer and add the grapes and bananas. Cook for 15 minutes.

2. Remove from heat and serve warm.

Serves 12

Marinated Fruit Bowl

12-ounce can pitted bing cherries and/or 1 large bunch dark purple grapes
2 cups sugar
Juice of 3 lemons (divided)
½ cup brandy or orange-flavored liqueur
5 large ripe pears, peeled and sliced
2 tart apples, peeled and sliced
3 Golden Delicious apples, peeled and sliced
3 navel oranges, peeled and sectioned
12 marshmallows, cut into 1-inch pieces
½ cup toasted nuts (cashews, pine nuts, or walnuts) for garnish
2 bananas (optional)

This dish may be spectacular or simple, depending on which fruits are in season. Fresh cherries are nice if you can get them. I also add several kiwi or berries for color and a little different flavor. Bananas are good too, but cannot be added until the last minute.

Microwave

1. Drain canned cherries and cut in half (or cut grapes in half and remove seeds) and place in a 6-quart bowl.

2. Place sugar, juice of 2 lemons, and 3 cups water in a microwave-safe container. Cook on high setting for 10 minutes or until bubbly. Turn to roast setting, cook 5 minutes longer. Add brandy and let cool.

3. Place pear and apple slices in a 2-quart microwave-safe baking dish with juice of 1 lemon and ½ cup water. Cover with vented plastic wrap and cook on high setting for 8 to 10 minutes. Drain, adding liquid to sugar syrup. Let cool.

4. Add pear and apple slices to cherries and grapes. Add orange sections and marshmallows. Add syrup and let marinate several hours or overnight.

5. Toast nuts by placing in a microwave-safe container on high setting for 3 minutes (stirring once) or until golden brown. Use as a garnish.

Conventional

In step 2, place the syrup ingredients in a medium saucepan. Simmer 25 minutes or until thick and syrupy. In step 3, cook the pears and apples, lemon juice and water, for 10 minutes in a 4-quart saucepan. In step 5, spread nuts on a cookie sheet, and toast in a preheated 375° oven for 15 to 20 minutes.

Serves 12

Desserts

Lemon Angel Pie

½ cup egg whites (4
large eggs), room
temperature
1 teaspoon vinegar
1 teaspoon vanilla (see
conversion table)
1¼ cups sugar

Filling

1¼ cups sugar
4 tablespoons potato
starch
Dash of salt
1¼ cups ice water
4 slightly beaten egg
yolks
Grated peel of 2 lemons
6 tablespoons lemon juice
2 tablespoon butter or
margarine

1. Preheat oven to 250° F. Grease a 9-inch pie plate.
2. With electric mixer, beat egg whites at medium speed until they are frothy and hold soft peaks. Add vinegar and vanilla and turn mixer to high. When eggs begin to hold a soft peak or when you begin to see the lines from the beaters in the egg whites, begin to add the sugar, about 2 tablespoons at a time. Beat thoroughly after each addition. Continue until all the sugar has been added and the egg whites are very stiff and glossy.
3. Spread meringue into pie plate, building up the sides and leaving the center flattened for the filling. Bake for 1 hour. Cool on cake rack for 1 hour.
4. While meringue is baking, make the filling. Combine sugar, potato starch, and salt in a medium saucepan. Gradually add ice water. Stir in egg yolks, lemon peel, and lemon juice. Cook and stir over medium heat until bubbly. Boil only one minute—no longer!
5. Remove from heat and stir in butter. Let cool 15 to 20 minutes.
6. Fill meringue shell, and garnish with toasted coconut or toasted almonds.

Serves 6 to 8

Italian Cassata

6 large eggs, separated
½ cup sugar
2 cups whipped cream
9 slices sponge cake
  (about 2″ x 3½″)
½ cup plus 1 teaspoon
  brandy
8 ounces semi-sweet
  chocolate
1 tablespoon strong
  coffee
½ cup chopped pecans
1 tablespoon grated
  orange peel

Chocolate Sauce

12 ounces semi-sweet
  chocolate
1 tablespoon brandy

Over the years we have had many interesting visitors. Dora Roth, who worked for the Israeli government, was one of them—she was vibrant, bright, and very giving. We had the opportunity to exchange recipes. Dora's dessert is very rich, but elegant and easy to make.

1. With electric mixer, beat egg whites at medium speed until they are frothy and hold soft peaks. Add the sugar, about 2 tablespoons at a time. Beat thoroughly after each addition. Continue until all the sugar has been added.

2. Beat yolks slightly and fold into whites. Whip cream until stiff and fold into egg mixture.

3. Brush cake with ½ cup brandy. Line the bottom and sides of a 10-inch springform pan with the slices.

4. Melt the chocolate with 1 teaspoon of brandy over warm water until smooth. Let cool.

5. Divide the egg mixture into 3 equal parts. Fold the chocolate into one part, the coffee into another part, and the pecans and grated orange peel into the third part.

6. Pour in the coffee layer first, then the orange layer, and finally the chocolate layer. Place in freezer for 4 hours or until firm.

7. Make the chocolate sauce by melting the chocolate with the brandy. Let cool.

8. Remove cassata from freezer 15 minutes before serving. Serve with chocolate sauce.

Serves 14 to 16

Trifle

1 cup raspberry or
   strawberry jam
1 sponge cake, sliced
   thick
½ cup slivered almonds
¾ cup semi-sweet
   Passover wine
1 cup heavy cream,
   whipped (or to taste)

Custard

1½ cups milk
1 cup heavy cream
¼ cup sugar
1 teaspoon vanilla (see
   conversion table)
1 teaspoon potato starch
5 egg yolks, beaten

This is a perfect way to use up some of your Passover sponge cake in an elegant and easy manner. You may substitute 2 packages (3 ounces each) Passover pudding mix for the custard.

1. Make the custard. Bring milk and cream to a boil in a double boiler. Remove from heat.

2. Combine sugar, vanilla, potato starch, and egg yolks. Add ¼ cup of hot milk/cream, beating well. Add remaining milk/cream and return to the double boiler. Stir over medium high heat until the custard becomes thick and creamy. Do not boil!

3. Cool custard slightly; pour in a bowl, cover, and refrigerate until well chilled, about 2 hours.

4. Thickly spread jam on the cake slices and arrange on the bottom of a souffle dish (a glass dish is especially pretty). Sprinkle evenly with the almonds. Add the wine and allow to soak thoroughly.

5. Pour custard over the cake and top with whipped cream. Garnish with fresh fruit or toasted slivered almonds, if desired. Refrigerate.

Serves 10 to 12

Sorbet (basic recipe)

⅔ cup sugar
⅔ cup water
3 cups of any pureed
    fresh fruit: berries,
    bananas, peaches, pears
1 tablespoon vanilla or
    almond flavoring or
    liqueur
1 egg white or 1 cup
    heavy cream (optional)

You can add an egg white (which makes the sorbet smoother) or cream (which makes it richer and smoother). You must still process and refreeze before serving.

Processor

1. Make a sugar syrup: combine sugar and water in a saucepan and cook over medium heat until sugar dissolves. (Don't let it come to boil.) Let cool.

2. Insert metal blade, and process the fruit for 1 minute. Add cooled syrup and flavoring and process until mixture is smooth. Pour into metal container and freeze.

3. Several hours before serving, remove from freezer. Break up to fit into work bowl. Process with metal blade, adding egg white or cream through feed tube while machine is running.

4. Return to metal bowl, cover, and refreeze. Let soften a little before serving.

Serves 6 to 8

Red Raspberry Sorbet

See Seder Menu #1 for recipe.

Chocolate Mousse

¼ cup sugar
4 tablespoons brandy
3½ ounces semi-sweet
   chocolate
2 egg whites
2 cups heavy cream,
   chilled

Microwave

1. Cook sugar and brandy in microwave for 2 minutes. Cool slightly. Melt chocolate in microwave for 2 minutes. Mix together and let cool.

2. Beat egg whites until stiff. Fold chocolate mixture into egg whites. (If chocolate mixture is too thick, thin with a teaspoon of brandy or boiling water.) Whip cream, and fold in.

3. Pour into serving dish. Chill in refrigerator about 3 hours or until set.

Conventional

In step 1, heat sugar and brandy in saucepan until sugar melts. Melt chocolate in double boiler.

Serves 6 to 8

Chocolate Raspberry Mousse

¼ cup sugar
⅓ cup red raspberry
   syrup
4 ounces bittersweet
   chocolate
2 egg whites
2 cups whipping cream,
   chilled

This is an easy make-ahead dessert. Doubling it for a crowd doesn't harm the flavor.

1. Cook sugar and syrup in a small saucepan over very low heat until sugar is dissolved; do not let turn brown. Let cool.

2. Melt the chocolate and add to the syrup. (If mixture seems too thick, add a teaspoon or two of boiling water or raspberry syrup.)

3. Beat egg whites until very stiff. Fold chocolate mixture into egg whites

4. Beat the whipping cream until stiff. Fold into chocolate mixture. Chill well before serving.

Serves 8 to 10

Cold Lemon Mousse

4 teaspoons unflavored
   Passover gelatin*
5 large eggs, separated
1¼ cups granulated
   sugar
Juice and peel of 2
   lemons
2 cups whipping cream,
   chilled
Strawberries for garnish

This is a light, airy dessert that will melt in your mouth!

1. Sprinkle the gelatin over ¼ cup hot water. Heat over moderate heat, stirring constantly until gelatin is completely dissolved. (You may also heat in a 2-cup microwave-safe measure in the microwave on high setting for 2 minutes, stirring after each minute.)

2. In the large bowl of the electric mixer, beat the egg whites until soft peaks form. Transfer to another bowl and set aside.

3. In the same bowl, beat the egg yolks and sugar on high speed until thick and lemon-colored (about 10 minutes). Add gelatin, lemon juice, and lemon peel, beating constantly until everything is well combined. Refrigerate about 30 minutes, or place in the freezer for 10 minutes, until mixture is the consistency of unbeaten egg whites.

4. Beat the whipping cream until stiff. Remove egg-yolk mixture from refrigerator and whisk in 2 tablespoons of the whipped cream. Fold in the beaten egg whites, then the remaining whipped cream.

5. Spoon into a 2-quart souffle dish or 12 individual stemmed glasses. Chill at least 4 hours. Garnish with fresh strawberries.

Serves 12

* Kosher gelatin gels differently from non-kosher gelatin. See conversion table.

Macaroon Delight

5 large eggs, separated
¾ cup matzah cake meal
¼ teaspoon baking soda
¼ teaspoon cream of tartar
1 cup finely ground almonds
1 cup sugar
1 teaspoon almond flavoring
½ cup red raspberry preserves
¼ cup red raspberry syrup
Confectioners' sugar (see conversion table) or whipped cream

1. Preheat oven to 325° F. Grease a 9-inch springform pan well.

2. Beat egg whites until stiff. Set aside.

3. Sift matzah cake meal; mix in ground almonds.

4. With electric mixer set on high, beat the egg yolks until thick and very light lemon in color; this may take 10 to 15 minutes. Continue beating, and add sugar gradually, then almond flavoring. Gradually add dry ingredients. Fold in egg whites. Pour into springform pan and bake for 1 hour.

5. Let cool for 10 minutes on a rack, then remove sides of pan. When cake has cooled completely, remove bottom of pan and cut cake in half horizontally.

6. Combine preserves and syrup and spread between layers. Sprinkle with confectioners' sugar or cover with whipped cream.

Serves 8 to 10

Passover Cream Puffs

½ cup matzah cake meal
½ cup potato starch
¼ teaspoon salt
1 cup water (or ½ cup water and ½ cup orange juice)
1 stick unsalted butter or margarine
½ teaspoon vanilla (see conversion table)
2 tablespoons sugar
4 eggs

For appetizers or lunch, you may fill puffs with tuna, chicken, or salmon salad.

Processor

1. Preheat oven to 375° F. Grease a large cookie sheet or cover it with greased aluminum foil.

2. Sift together cake meal, potato starch, and salt. Set aside.

3. Place water, butter, vanilla, and sugar in saucepan. Let come to a boil, stirring occasionally. Remove from heat as soon as butter melts, and add sifted ingredients all at once. Stir well with wooden spoon until mixture begins to form a ball and pulls away from sides of pan.

4. Return to heat for 1 to 2 minutes and stir constantly to extract all moisture. Cool 5 minutes.

5. Insert metal blade. Place dough in work bowl. Add eggs all at once, and pulse several times until eggs are mixed well into dough and a smooth, shiny ball begins to form. Scrape down ingredients at least once between pulses. The dough is now ready. (It will keep up to 24 hours in the refrigerator.)

6. Fill a pastry bag with the dough and force through a #6 tube into mounds onto the cookie sheet, 2 inches apart. Or wet your hands with cold water and form balls.

7. Bake for 10 minutes. Reduce heat to 325°. Poke small air hole in each puff with tip of sharp knife and bake 40 to 50 minutes longer, or until golden brown. Remove to cake rack to cool.

8. To assemble cream puffs, split in half and pull out soft insides, then place 1 large tablespoon of filling on bottom half. Cover with top and ice with chocolate glaze. Refrigerate several hours before serving.

Conventional

In step 5, use a portable or rotary mixer; add eggs to saucepan one at a time, beating well after each addition; keep beating until dough becomes smooth and shiny.

Makes 8 to 10 large, or 12 to 16 small puffs

Note: You may freeze, unfilled, for future use. Defrost in a 425° oven for 5 minutes.

Lemon Filling

¾ cup sugar
2 tablespoons potato starch
Dash of salt
¾ cup ice water
2 slightly beaten egg yolks
Grated peel of 1 lemon
3 tablespoons lemon juice
1 tablespoon butter or margarine

Combine sugar, potato starch, and salt in a medium saucepan. Gradually add ice water. Stir in egg yolk, lemon peel, and lemon juice. Cook and stir over medium heat until bubbly. Boil only one minute—no longer! Remove from heat and stir in butter. Let cool 15 to 20 minutes. Fills 8 to 10 large or 12 to 16 small puffs.

Mocha Filling

2 ounces semi-sweet chocolate
2 cups whipping cream, chilled
2 tablespoons sugar
¼ teaspoon instant coffee

Melt chocolate (microwave on medium setting for 2 minutes, or heat in double boiler over hot water). Whip cream with sugar and coffee until stiff. Fold in melted chocolate. Fills 8 to 10 large or 12 to 16 small puffs.

Chocolate Glaze

4 ounces semi-sweet chocolate
¼ cup water

Bring chocolate and water to a boil. Spread small amount immediately on each cream puff. Refrigerate to set.

Chocolate Marshmallow Surprise

¼ cup butter
3½ cups Passover
  marshmallows
1 cup nuts (walnuts or
  almonds)
5 cups matzah farfel
1 cup raisins
½ teaspoon cinnamon
6 ounces chocolate (I
  prefer semi-sweet
  chocolate bars)

A great Passover confection for the young set!

1. Butter a 9 x 13 pan and set aside. Melt butter over low heat. Add marshmallows and stir until melted. Remove from heat.

2. With the processor fitted with the metal blade, chop nuts with quick pulses until fine. (Or chop nuts by hand.) Add half the nuts to the melted marshmallows. Reserve the remaining nuts for garnish.

3. Stir matzah farfel, raisins, and cinnamon into marshmallow mixture. Spread evenly in the pan with wet hands, and pat down.

4. Melt the chocolate, and drizzle it over the farfel. Sprinkle with reserved nuts. Refrigerate for about 15 minutes or until chocolate has set. Cut into squares.

Makes about 4 dozen

Index

Wine *(continued)*
  White, with Boston Scrod and
    Vegetables, 114

Y

Yogurt
  Apricot Soup, 68

with Fish Fillets, 112

Z

Zeroa, 9
Zucchini, 88
  Julienne Vegetables, 87
  Souffle, 110